Online Therapy – Reading Between the lines.

(and solution-focused)

A practical NLP based guide to online counselling and therapy skills.

Jethro Adlington.

ISBN13 9781904312741

Published in the UK by
MX Publishing,
335, Princess Park Manor, Royal Drive, London, N11 3GX
www.mxpublishing.co.uk

Acknowledgements.

I would like to thank Jeni. B, for her feedback, particularly with regard to the "reading cures" chapter. I would also like to thank Geraldine. W, for her proof reading skills, and also Janice. G, for her technical help. I would like to thank Mark, Man, Baz, Ali, Geraldine and Hag. And most of all, I would like to say that I could not have even started this journey without the unswerving support of Alifib, my wife.

Disclaimer.

All persons and characters defined in this publication, with the exception of the author, are fictitious, and any resemblance to real persons, either living or dead, is purely coincidental.

Contents.

Online Therapy: Reading between the lines.

When I first started working professionally as an online therapist, there were not too many published books on the subject of online counselling and therapy. As I obtained the available books, I was aware that most of them gave help, advice and instruction on the essentials of online therapy; the type of computer system required and relevant encryption software, how to set up assessment and contracting, confidentiality as well as legal and financial implications etc.

As I was working as a beginner from "scratch", I found these books highly useful, as they enabled me to set up the most practicable environment for working as a therapist online. They also showed me "what" to do in terms of setting up a legal and ethical framework, which was essential. However, as I was working professionally as an online therapist, I found that many of the books did not have significant sections on the *skills* that could be used when working online.

As I continued with my studies into online therapy, I progressed from certificate level, through to obtaining a diploma in online counselling. The training I received was excellent and it allowed me to connect with other therapists working online as well as being supported and encouraged by the tutors along the way.

Whilst I was undertaking my online training, I was also worked in an educational setting in a university, providing online counselling for students that could not physically attend face-to-face sessions or had decided, perhaps due to their issues, that online counselling was more suitable for them. For me, this was an invaluable experience, as it allowed me to not only set up and utilise all the learning I had acquired from textbooks and the training courses, but also (and perhaps most important too), it allowed me to build on my *skills;* the **"how"** I work online.

Prior to working online, I had trained as an NLP psychotherapist, (neurolinguistic programming) and as I worked online, I found myself "picking out" a range of linguistic patterns in the clients' emails and chat exchanges. As I started to "read between the lines", to recognise and respond to these patterns, I noticed that the feedback from ex clients was very positive.

Whilst I was still working towards my online counselling diploma, I interacted with other online therapists and as I exchanged ideas with them about how we worked online, I realised that virtually no one had had any contact with NLP and how it could be used in online work.

So I decided to write this book as a "second level" publication. A book for counsellors and therapists that may already be working online and already know about "what to do", and now want to move on to a second level, where they can use the NLP approaches discussed in this book, in a way that is right for them, so that they can do "how" they do their online therapy skills, even better.

This book therefore focuses mainly on a range of counselling and therapy *skills* that can be employed when working online.

Of course, the book can also be useful to someone who is *contemplating* a move towards working as an online therapist, as the skills discussed here can also be used in parallel with the core requirements for working online.

Jethro Adlington. U.K.C.P. accredited N.L.Pt.C.A. psychotherapist.

Jethro has 20 years experience working as a psychotherapist and trainer. His experience has been based in the voluntary sector, industry, and private practice. He has also worked as a counsellor in college and university settings. In 1998, whilst working as a volunteer therapist in a hospital setting in the USA, Jethro set up a private online practice for UK residents, and in 2003 he helped pilot and run an online counselling scheme in a university setting. He qualified as a NLP trainer in 1997 and as an accredited NLPtCA psychotherapist in 1998.

"This engaging book takes the reader on a journey into language, exploring its use in online therapy. Jethro imbues his subject with infectious enthusiasm and makes his points in a lively and refreshing way through a series of online workshops. This book will benefit anyone who already works with words and should be required reading for anyone planning to work online as a psychological therapist."

Gill Jones, Director, Online Training for Counsellors Ltd., Past Chairman, Association for Counselling and Therapy Online.

"Jethro has provided a useful contribution to the developing field of online therapy. This book is an enjoyable and worthwhile read and a must for any therapist considering embarking on this approach to therapy. Full of practical examples and easy to understand references I would highly recommend this book to therapists from a diverse range of disciplines who want to get the most out of their online work with clients."

Lisa Wake, Awaken Consulting and Training Services Ltd
Former Chair of UKCP
Author of Neurolinguistic Psychotherapy: A Postmodern Perspective; Routledge (2008), & The Role of Brief Therapy in Attachment Disorders: Karnac (in press)

Chapter 1.

How do we build rapport online?

Jethro: Welcome to the world of digital communication. Did you all manage to log on without any problems?

Man: I'm here.

Ali: Me too.

Hag: Ditto.

Baz: Here I am.

Geraldine: Yes, I just made it ☺

Mark: Well I think you got here before me, so I'm last but not least LOL.

Jethro: That's good. So, if you are already working as an online therapist and are using email exchange or a chat style format, then you will be truly working in a digital world...

If you are also working as a face-to-face therapist, then you will experience your client talking and making conversation. You will therefore experience the tone of voice used by the client. This is an analogue form of communicating as voice tone can increase or decrease in volume; it can rise or fall in pitch. Voice tone can have an infinite variation in tone.

Hag: Yes I can see why you call that analogue. One example I often consider is that a "dimmer" switch on a light is analogue, as it can produce a variety of light levels, depending on how the dimmer is set, but a normal light switch is digital, as it has two options – on and off.

Jethro: I like that example Hag. When working face-to-face you will also be aware of the client's body language and body language can have an infinite number of variances; an arm can move a little or a lot, skin tone can change from a slight pink to a full red blush, and so body language is also an analogue form of communication...

However, when you are working solely with text, then these small, analogue changes are not there, so you are really working digitally when you work with text, so let's explore our digital world and see how we can utilise it as therapists...

Online therapy, as a medium for therapeutic change is relatively new, and my remit over the period of these workshops is to look at how an online counsellor can use a series of linguistic skills in order to facilitate change in the client. This already presupposes that the people in this "room" already have some skills, training and experience in online counselling and wish to improve those skills, so that they will have more choice in the way they work...

As this workshop is about new skills for online counsellors, I won't be looking at the historical perspectives and how online counselling came into existence. I won't dwell on the technology required in order to carry out online counselling or how you will carry out assessment and referral procedures or ethical considerations...

Instead, this workshop is about how you can take the series of skills that we will explore, and introduce them in your work...

We will explore how you can use these skills when working with email exchange as well as in a chat format. We will also explore where some of the skills may favour one of those modes of communication...

So let's look at a range of concepts and skills when working online, either **synchronously** or **asynchronously...**

But before we go further, I would like to rewind back to those two words that I just used, because I need to check that you all understand what I mean by working synchronously and asynchronously....

Man: Well I understand that working asynchronously is the term generally applied to email exchange and the word synchronously is applied to chat exchanges...

Yes, that's about it. So let's just put that here now so you can all see that...

Asynchronous = email exchange.

Synchronous = Chat.

I will refer to these two modes of exchange as we progress and so it's important that you all know the difference now...

One of the most misquoted pieces of research is probably the work carried out by Albert Mehrabian on verbal and non-verbal communication. Many professionals from psychotherapists, to human communication experts, say that ***all*** communication is made up of 55% body language, 38% tonality and only 7% is actually related to the words that were used...

Of course this is not the case in all situations and these percentages are not applicable in email or text exchange...

However, online communication, whether it is by email exchange or by using a chat format, does not allow the therapist or the client to have access to body language or tonality at all, and therefore the mode of communication is **100% connected to the actual words that are laid out on the page...**

So, if all we online therapists have to go on is the text itself, then if we can see a little deeper into the text and respond with more choices, then that's bound to be helpful to you now...

Consider building rapport for instance. Have any of you had any experience of building rapport when working face-to- face or in a social setting?

Man: I've read quite a few books about building rapport in face-to-face situations.

Jethro: Go on please.

Man: Well as far as I can remember, the basic premise for being able to build rapport in a face-to-face relationship is first of all to match the person you are with.

Jethro: So, if you match the person's body language, their speech, their posture, their breathing, after a while, whether it's a few minutes or many hours, you will eventually gain rapport?

Man: Well that's the theory.

Jethro: And how do you test to see if you have reached a state of rapport with someone you are with, when working face-to-face?

Man: Well from what I have read, and to some extent from my personal experience, a person can match the other person until he or she thinks rapport has been achieved. To test to see if rapport has been achieved, the person will "lead" by making a gesture or a change in body posture, and then check out to see if the other person "follows". If the person follows, then there is a good chance that they are on the way to reaching rapport.

Jethro: In a nutshell, I agree that's basically what a lot of books will state about building rapport when "face-to-face", and so let's keep it at that for now…

Let's consider working online and how different rapport building can be. Here is the very first line of an email that you may receive from a client. I'm thinking about the way the client addresses you…

Dear Jethro

Hiya Jethro

Hiya

Jethro: Or perhaps there is no introduction, but with the client going directly into the message. How would you respond?

Man: Well I would respond like this. If the client were "Mike" I would reply...

Intro	Reply
Dear Jethro	Dear Mike
Hiya Jethro	Hiya Mike
Hiya	Hiya
No intro	No intro

Jethro: So you are matching their introduction with a parallel response.

Man: Yes that's it in a nutshell.

Ali: I agree with all of those except the last one. If someone emailed me and did not give an introduction, I would still reply with "Hello Mike" because that's my way of saying that I recognise that they are "with me".

Geraldine: Yes, me too. I like to think that by responding to them and using their name when they do not give an introduction, allows me to say to them "I recognise you".

Jethro: So you are both saying that mirroring can work in the case where the client provides an introduction, but if there is no introduction, then you would prefer to address the client by name to show that you have recognised them.

Baz: And for me the same would apply when signing off.

Geraldine: Yes, I was just about to say that. I would mirror their "sign off" and if they didn't use their name when signing off, I would still use mine, as a way of letting them know who I am and the fact that I have a presence.

Jethro: Yes I can mirror what you are saying there. By responding that way, you are sending a message to the client that says that they exist, and that you exist too. By using names that way, you are starting to build on the process of making the client and therapist "real".

Hag: Something that is important when there are so few cues to the identity of the users.

Jethro: I agree. There are no "head nod" moments in online work, so the best way to build rapport, the best way to create a head nod is to feedback to the client that you know that they are real, and that what they are saying has been heard.

Man: Yes, if I were working face-to-face I would use a head nod to indicate that I had heard the client. How would I do this online?

Jethro: Paraphrasing what the client says in the email is a good way to do this. It's the digital equivalent of the head nod ☺

Let's look at this email and a head nod response...

Dear Therapist

I know that I should be able to focus on my studies but I'm really not able to as I have so many financial problems as well as having a boyfriend that just won't let me have any time to myself. If I am at home, he assumes I am with someone else and so texts me constantly. When I don't reply he phones and then we argue so he calls around and then I get no work done.

Client.

Dear Client

When I read over your email I started to understand what you might be experiencing in your life. It sounds as if you would really like to work hard on your studies but your concerns over your finances and the way your boyfriend is behaving is affecting your ability to focus on your work. I felt that I had to read over what you wrote about how your relationship with your boyfriend is affecting you, so I could be clear in my response to you.

Therapist.

Jethro: I hope you can see that the response paraphrases the client's issues in their email and therefore starts to let the client know that the therapist is listening to them. As you know, when a person believes they are being listened to, it gives them a feeling of trust and that helps build up rapport.

Mark: Do you have any other lines that a therapist may use to let the client know they have been heard?

Jethro: I'm open to suggestions.

Mark: How about "I found myself nodding in agreement".

Jethro: Well that's a pretty good text based representation of a head nod.

Hag: At the end of my first email I like to write "We have made a start".

Ali: Oooh! I like that. It seems to indicate to the client that there will be more emails to follow and I think that's a great way to maintain client contact.

Baz: Sometimes I put my thoughts in brackets to the client, such as ...

(Taking time here to think about what to put next)...

 And...

(Reading over this section again)...

 I think that's a good way to let my client know that I am listening to them and it makes me more real as I can even add physical elements to it such as...

(Looking puzzled here) etc.

Jethro: Good points Baz. We can all use a combination of these responses to let the client know we are real and then go on to use them to build rapport. I have, however, seen some email responses where the response to the client is *only* paraphrasing and not moving on to anything else. I feel that paraphrasing is a great tool for rapport building and it works better if it is incorporated into goal achievement too. We can explore this exciting element of working online in a later session.

Hag: Sounds like you are building expectation LOL.

Jethro: I will tell you later.

Hag: ☺

Jethro: Let me just ask you all this question...

If you received a text from a new client and the text style, irrespective of the content of the email, looked like this.

I am not feeling too good today

Ali: I would instantly wonder why the client decided to use such a font.

Man: I would think that he dresses like Charles Dickens and writes his emails by candlelight LOL.

Jethro: Ok so the type of font that a client uses and the type of font that you use could have an impact. It's worth considering the type of font you use in response to a client, so here are some rhetorical questions for you...

In the example above, what would you do if a client used that text?

How would you approach such a situation?

How could you use text to gain rapport?

If we look at the pacing and leading model, then would a good way to build rapport be to start off using their font, and then slowly move to your own, less florid font?

Man: I can already see that this can get complicated.

Jethro: Yes, and that's why were talking about this, so that even if you do not know the answers now, it's important that you at least consider this when you are working online.

Man: Okay what would you do?

Jethro: Well he may be dressed like Charles Dickens or he may not, but **he gets something positive out of using such a font**. If I was working with email exchange I would use my normal font, which just happens to be the font I'm using here, but I would very **occasionally** drop in a word or two of the client's font. I might sign off in their font or quote back their words in the font they originally used...

For example...

> And I'm sure that we can spend some time emailing each other, exploring, testing and examining how things can be different.
>
> Until next week
>
> Jethro

Jethro: So another aspect you may want to consider is to make sure that you use the client's font when you are cutting and pasting sections of the client's text back to them...

> Therapist: Paul, you mentioned that you liked to sit alone in your room and cry, and I wondered if that was what you really liked to do?

Man: And now I have seen that on the screen I guess that text size can make a difference too.

Jethro: Text size may be an issue for the client if he or she is partially sighted, so it's always good to check that out if you get really large text in an email. Also, if you designate that a client has to send a limit of e.g. a page of work to you, and then they may use really small text size if they want to say more per page.

Man: that's cheating LOL.

Jethro: Well it's just their way of getting value for money. Personally I'd go for a contract that stipulated word count rather than page length. What else can vary in an email from a client?

Ali: Text colour.

Jethro: Yes, that's a good one.

Geraldine: I worked with a client that used colour in a very dramatic way. He used green for envy and red for love and purple for rage.

Jethro: Yes and also I wonder if the use of colour can help with rapport building too. If a client uses colours perhaps you could drop some colour into your letters too.

Man: I think I would follow the model of dropping in little bits of colour in my text and see if they take up the gauntlet and use colour when they reply, I feel that could show that I was building rapport with a client.

Baz: What about using images to build rapport?

Jethro: Yes, a good one. Once I worked with a person who was setting up her own cosmetics business. After a while she sent me a piece of clip art when she was referring to her business.

Baz: And I guess you used it?

Jethro: Yes I responded by asking a question in my email and added the logo from the clip art she had used. The logo kept appearing in her emails from then on, and when I referred to her business I mirrored the logo. I feel that could indicate that there is some sort of mutual sharing and an increase in rapport don't you think?

Baz: And what about the use of underlining and italics?

Jethro: Any comments from others about this?

Hag: Well underlining is another, perhaps more subtle way to show emphasis, and I like to use italics as a way of feeding back text to the client.

Jethro: So you would use italics to cut and paste the client's text and feed it back to them as if they had said it, like a quote.

Hag: Yes.

Jethro: You mean like this...

So Rundeep, in your last email you said *"If I go away with him and my family find out then I will be disowned by them all and my father may even get violent"*. Have you any evidence to suggest that your father will act in a violent way to you?

Hag: Yes, that's what I like to do.

Jethro: Me too, and I still prefer to use their original font, only italicised. I feel that its shows clearly that you are using the client's direct quotes from a previous email. It does send a message to the client that you have taken the time to look at what they actually wrote, so it could be a rapport builder.

Hag: One other aspect where rapport can be built up or even broken down is in the use of capital letters.

Jethro: Please continue.

Hag: Well in the world of sending text messages and emails, the use of capital letters can mean that the person sending the message is shouting.

Jethro: YES I HEAR WHAT YOU SAY. AND I AGREE WITH YOU SO PERHAPS YOU WOULDN'T WANT TO CONSTRUCT YOUR EMAILS LIKE THIS, OR USE CAPITALS FOR ONLINE CHAT. HOWEVER, IF YOU CONSTANTLY USE CAPITALS FROM THE START OF YOUR EMAILS THEN HOW WOULD YOU ACTUALLY "SHOUT" OR EMPHASISE WORDS?

Hag: LOL.

Jethro: Well I like to have the capital letters as a tool for emphasis and perhaps it can be really useful in the right context...

When I see larger text, I assume it means LOUDER VOLUME and not a change in tonality. Again, this is not an analogue shift but a digital one as the size of the font is not covered by an infinite range of choices but by the font sizes allocated on the computer so mine can do a 14 point word and a 16 point word, but it does not have the ability to do a 15 point, or anything in between. If it could do so, then I would say that VOLUME could be seen as analogue but it's not on my PC now.

Hag: Nor mine either.

Jethro: Here's an example...

Jane, I read in your email that you never do anything right. Are you sure that you NEVER do ANYTHING right?

Mark: Well it could still be seen as shouting.

Jethro: I agree and sometimes shouting in text can be the best way to emphasise a point. I think it's important to use capitals for emphasis, and it's equally important to use them sparingly. It's a little like swearing, the less you use it, the more powerful it is when you do...!

However, it may be that when you are working online, you may not receive a large number of emails with unusual fonts, colours and graphics etc. I think it's worth exploring these possibilities, as we have done so today, as it can allow you to think about the fact that it can happen, and therefore its worthwhile to consider how you would respond if it did.

Mark: I would say, that when I work face-to-face, I do not get that many psychotic clients but I'm glad I had done some training when it happened!

Jethro: An interesting comparison and I can see your point. It's better to have explored this aspect of online work so you can have a little insight into what may happen...

Do you think that you could build rapport online by matching the **verbal predicates** in their text?

Mark: Can you define what you mean by verbal predicates?

Jethro: Of course, but before I do that I will need to talk to you about...

Representational systems in language.

Most people have the five senses of **sight, hearing, smell, touch and taste.** I'm assuming that no one would disagree that these senses allow us to make sense of the world. Is that a pun? Sorry, bad joke...

Your clients may use words that link to these senses, for instance **visual** words may include sentences like...

I can't see my way out of here

My future looks dark

Life can be a bit of a blur to me sometimes

He is a black and white thinker

Let's focus on the problem here

You may get **auditory** words in sentences such as...

I find he is a great sounding board

Word for word he was better

I could easily tune into what she had to say

And of course there are **feelings or kinaesthetic** phrases too, such as...

I feel lost

We are out of touch with each other

I want to grasp it but I can't

We can make contact next week

If you can match these predicates in your replies, then you will be using choice in your responses to aid rapport? Here's an example...

Client: I know that I have a vision for the future but most of the time I just can't get hold of it.

Therapist Response 1: So when you can see what you need, then you will be able to grasp things more easily?

Therapist response 2: So when you are more tuned into what you need then you will be seeing things more easily?

Client: He just cannot make contact in the way I would like him to. I don't want him to echo my problems at all

Therapist Response 1: Its feels like you both need to be able to hear each other.

Therapist Response 2: It's clear that you both need to keep in touch.

Mark: I had a feeling of being more connected with response 1 in both cases.

Hag: I put myself in the place of the client and pretended I was saying those things to my therapist. I also felt that response 1 felt better on both occasions.

Jethro: Well that's good feedback but don't just take my word for it, I would like you to test it for yourselves. You can create a series of "client" statements that have visual, auditory and kinaesthetic messages on them and then produce two "response statements", one of which matches the predicates in the client statement and another that does not. Then ask a selection of people to pretend in their heads to be the client, saying either internally to themselves "as if" they were saying it to the therapist. Then get the person to decide which of the two responses they felt more connected with. Send me your results please LOL...

OK so we can consider the choice of matching predicates in language patterns to build rapport, is their anything else we can match if we want to build rapport online, either by email exchange or via synchronous chat...?

It's rather silent out there so I will ask you to think about it before we continue. Also if you have any questions, now would be a good time to ask.

Mark: When I write to a client in email and ask a question, I sometimes don't get an answer to the question, and that's frustrating for me as the answer would have helped me a lot in finding out about the client a little more.

Jethro: Well, clients may be in a different psychological state when sending and receiving emails. If you think about it, a client may get into a certain frame of mind or "state" when sending emails and then when they read your email response, they may not be in the same frame of mind. This doesn't apply to text exchanges, but to emails only. Also, when a client is constructing an email, its impossible to tell how they have constructed it. They may have taken days to produce the final email that you receive. It may have been spell checked and cut and pasted many times. They may have taken lots of care over its construction and you will not know that.

Man: Hmmm, never thought of that.

Jethro: So if they take ages to construct an email, they may be better "senders" than "receivers" and only glance at the email you send them. If you feel that you are not getting responses to your questions, then I would suggest that you consider the following as a way of increasing the chance of a client responding to a question you have sent to them asynchronously.
How to increase the chances of getting a response to your question when working asynchronously...

Write less in response so that your response focuses on the questions you really need answering...

Make sure that you do not put your questions in the main body of your text but separate the question from the text...

Highlight the question in bold...

Indicate you want a reply...

Consider these two replies...

Hello John

I understand from your email that you have several issues with your partner that concern you, and I'm wondering what they could be? I also read in your email that you also feel anxious when you are at work. Could you let me know what makes you anxious at work? I read that you have signed up for a course suggested by your doctor do you know what type of course that is?

And...

Hello John

I understand that you have several issues with your partner that concerns you.
John, I would like to know a little more about the issues that are bothering you

Could you write back and let me know specifically what types of issues are bothering you?

You also wrote and said that you get anxious at work.

Could you let me know just exactly what you believe is making you anxious at work?

Also John I would really appreciate it if you could let me know a little more about the course you have signed up for.

Could you let me know a little more about the course in your next reply to me?

Ali: The first example is very similar to the way I write, and I'm wondering if that's why I don't always get an answer to my questions.

Man: Yes it's difficult to know in the first example whether the questions are rhetorical or not.

Jethro: So if you want to increase your chances of the client replying to your questions, it's certainly worthwhile considering those options.

Mark: Yes, I like that. It's simple but effective. I could tell in the second example just exactly what the therapist wanted.

Jethro: So let's end there for today, and we can continue tomorrow, exploring how we can build rapport and a deeper sense of trust with our clients, because if resistance is due to the client and therapist not having enough rapport, then building rapport online is a very worthwhile and useful skill for us to master.

Chapter 2.

How do we build more rapport online?

Jethro: Well I can see that you have all logged on in good time.

Ali: Yes I think we were all here before you ☺

Jethro: Well I was here, but lurking invisibly LOL.

Hag: Are we going to continue today looking at building rapport?

Jethro: Yes Hag lets do that...

So here's a question to you all...

What's really important to you?

Ali: My children, to be seen as a good mother.

Hag: Being honest and truthful.

Jethro: Ok that's good. One way of looking at this is explore what I call the "gravestone test". Can I have a volunteer in the group?

Baz: Didn't someone say "never volunteer" LOL.

Jethro: Ok Baz, let's assume that you have the amazing opportunity to design your own gravestone. Don't worry Baz, I don't think you will need it whilst you're on the course but we could save it for you afterwards.

Baz: LOL.

Jethro: if you could design a gravestone and it said on it...

Here lies Baz he was _____

What would you like more than anything to be in those spaces? What words could really define what was important to you when you were alive?

Baz: He was a kind, generous guy.

Jethro: Ok, thanks Baz...

Here lies Baz he was a kind generous guy.

So Baz I guess that being a kind, generous, *living* guy is also important to you too.

Baz: Yep, that's me all right.

Jethro: Baz, thank you for your help. Could it be then that we have discovered some aspects of what is important to Baz...?

When we are working online, and we want to build that relationship with our clients, I would like you to consider the concept of being able to discover their values or what things are important to them. If you can do that, you then may feel that you could match those values in your responses to the client. This could give you more choice as to how you build rapport with a client. Shall we look at an example...?

Let's start with an example from a piece of synchronous chat. In synchronous chat, the number of words typed in one exchange is shorter than in an asynchronous email exchange...

Client: I want to quit my job because I hate it but I cannot do that because I have a family to support.

Therapist: John, what aspects of your life are really important to you?

Client: Well, making money.

Therapist: And what would making money do for you?

Client: Well it would make me feel more secure.

Therapist: So being secure is important to you.

Client: Yes, that's why I feel I need to make money, to make myself feel secure.

Therapist: I know that a lot of people like to feel secure in their lifestyle.

Jethro: So in order to find out what a person's values are, one option is to ask the direct question...

"What is important to you in your job?"
"What is important to you in this relationship?"
"What sorts of things are really important to you in your life?"

You can get a series of responses such as...

Going for a walk every day

Health

Cycling to work

Buying gifts for people

Honesty

You will notice that some of these responses here are actually behaviours, things that people do. If you ask a person "what is important to you" and you get a behaviour response then you can **chunk up** to the value by asking...

"And what does that do for you?"

Here's another example...

Therapist: What then, is really important to you in your relationship with you family and friends?

Client: To make sure I visit them all regularly.

Therapist: And what would visiting them all regularly do for you?

Client: I would be supportive.

Therapist: So it's important to you that you are supportive.

Client: Yes that's it.

Therapist: Many people like to feel that they can support their friends and family.

Jethro: At this point remember we are looking at matching values to build rapport with a client, and matching values is one way of doing that...

It's important to say that at this point we are matching values as a way of **building rapport and not as a way of entering into a therapeutic intervention to determine whether the values expressed are useful or not**. In fact, often people will enter into therapy because they have conflicting values or they do not even know what their values are, as many values tend to be out of conscious awareness.

Ali: You are therefore saying, that in order to build rapport, you can match the clients' values, but what if you feel that the value that the client lists as important is in some way damaging the client?

Jethro: Excellent! I was about to open up this aspect of the discussion, so you read my mind. If you want to match values in text after you have determined them, you could match them either by building a generalisation that the value expressed is one that is shared by others, or you could be more specific and state that you actually share this value. This is essentially matching values to build rapport. Of course this means a certain element of self-disclosure. If you are going to self disclose, then I would ask you to consider what could be gained from that disclosure that could be positive for the client?

Here are a few examples...

Therapist: So what's really important in the way you are with your brother?

Client: That he knows that I will do what I say.

Therapist: And what would that do for you.

Client: He would trust me.

Therapist: So trust is important to you.

Client: Yes it is
.
Therapist: I read somewhere that trust is the glue in a relationship and I felt that was a very powerful statement, what do you think?

Client: Yes trust is what keeps us together.

Jethro: So I asked the question...

"What's really important to you?" as a way of eliciting his values...

He gave me a response that was essentially about how he wanted to behave with his brother "That he knows I will do what I say"...

As this was a behavioural response I chunked up to a higher level by asking him "What would that do for you?"...

He responded by saying "He would trust me"...

I then went on to match his value of trust, not directly but indirectly by saying...

"I had read somewhere that trust is the glue in a relationship"

The client agreed.

Geraldine: And what if you didn't agree with the person's values?

Jethro: Mmmm... Shall we role-play that one?

Geraldine: okay.

Jethro: Let me start with the first question.

Geraldine: I'm ready.

Jethro: Okay Geraldine, can you think of a context for my first question?

Geraldine: Yes it's about work.

Jethro: So what's really important for you about how you behave at work?

Geraldine: To be able to get people to do what I want, even if I know there is no point in what I am asking them to do.

Jethro: So you want to be able to get people to do what you want, even though there is no point in it, and what does that do for you?

Geraldine: It makes me feel powerful.

Jethro: So feeling powerful is important to you.

Geraldine: Yes I love to feel powerful.

Jethro: Okay so at this point we have elicited that a value you have is to feel powerful, and in itself that is not a problem, so I won't want to mismatch that. At this point I think that you may have also given me a belief about yourself. The belief is...

When I give people pointless tasks it makes me feel powerful.

So my response would be...

I hear that you like to feel **powerful** and I guess that allows you to have **more choice** in the way you relate to your staff. **I know that feeling powerful and being able to have choices can make a person feel good.** I did find myself focusing on those people that were **being forced to do pointless tasks** and I wondered if you could **feel even more powerful** if you were to use your skills to give them some **really useful** things to do that would make them **feel good about themselves** but also **allow you to still feel powerful at the same time?**

Geraldine: Now I am reading that I feel that you have still matched my value of "power", but you have linked it to "choice". You have challenged my behaviour but not my value. I still feel a sense of connectedness here.

Jethro: That's good feedback Geraldine, thank you...

Remember, that we are still exploring ways of building rapport and matching values is one way of doing that. We will be looking at values from a different perspective later in the course and then we shall be looking at working with values online, in a therapeutic way...

So, simply speaking, we have looked at not only how to match a value, but also how to get it in the first place...

Values are important because they are really the gears that drive our behaviours. Whatever you may undertake, what type of behaviour you carry out, you will be doing it do satisfy a value of yours. I am here at the moment because it is important for me to let others know about online counselling and language...

So now we have touched on matching values as a way of building rapport in text communicating, I would like you to consider this question….

What is a belief?

Man: Something you believe in.

Jethro: Well yes that is true, but as you have used the word believe in your response I would then have to ask, "How do you know when you believe in something ".

Man: When I think that what I believe in is true.

Jethro: Yes, yes, that's closer I guess to what I am thinking about, anyone care to add to this?

Ali: So a belief is something that you feel is true for you.

Jethro: Yes I like that, it's pretty much a definition we can go with...

A belief is something we feel that is true for us.

So my follow up question is "How do you know when you have a belief?"

Hag: We feel it.

Jethro: Well yes there is a physiological link between beliefs and feelings, I guess that is why I get so angry when people tell me that Santa Claus does not exist, it's just hard wired into my belief system that any suggestion that he doesn't exist, just cranks up my adrenalin….

As we are at a workshop looking at language and online therapy, then how can we recognise a belief that has been expressed in text?

It's gone a little quiet out there, so let me continue. If you read an email or were involved in Internet chat with a client do you think they would say...?

"I **believe** I am a bad father"

Baz: I think it is unlikely that they would actually use the word believe.

Jethro: Yes, so they would say I am a bad father and the belief would be in there covertly....

If that is the case, then how many belief statements are in the examples below?

I fell over the cat

When my mother phones me it's because she wants more money

I have a new coat

Men are better car drivers than women

I am a professor

Too many cooks spoil the broth...

In written language beliefs are often expressed, not overtly such as "I believe that too many cooks spoil the broth" but in two covert forms. These two ways of expressing beliefs are....

This means that.

Or

This causes that.

Now look at the statements above and see if you can spot a "this means that" or a "this causes that" in the above statements.

Man: When my mother phones it means she wants more money.

Baz: Too many cooks will cause the broth to be spoiled.

Man: Being a man means you are a better driver than a woman.

Hag: Well the last one is a false belief for sure LOL.

Jethro: Let me say a word about beliefs here. At the moment we are talking about matching a person's belief in order to build rapport online. Of course as you are therapists, you may not feel that you will want to match your client's beliefs, because in essence they may be presenting beliefs that are limiting or damaging to them, so it's not really a good therapeutic alliance if you start to match the very beliefs that are not helping the client. Later on in the workshop we will be looking at how you can change a person's limiting belief. Can you imagine how that could be if you could recognise a belief in text, and then reply to the person holding that belief in a way that they were able to reassess the belief from the new perspective, and then perhaps their belief will have changed. So at this point in the workshop I want you to be aware that...

Matching a person's belief is a great way to build rapport.
Beliefs are not always stated in text in the form "I believe in..."

They are often stated in text in the form of

This means that

This causes that

As a therapist you will have to consider whether you want to match the client's beliefs or not.

Mark: But we wouldn't want to match a client's irrational and limiting belief.

Jethro: Good point. If the client has a belief that shows that both sides of the "equation" are "ok" for the client, then it's likely that matching it will be a good way to build rapport...
For example...

When my children come home, I feel so happy.

As this is an "ok causes ok", then I would think that matching the belief, as a way of building rapport is worthwhile...

Yes I understand that having your children home would lead you to feeling happy.

Jethro: If either side of the "equation" are "not ok", then I would not match the belief, as it would probably be limiting in some way for the client...

I know that this illness will ruin my life.

I'm suffering and he's happy now.

Ali: I can see that the "not ok" section would not be good to match there.

Jethro: We can explore how to work with that type of belief later...

And finally there is another aspect of rapport building that you may wish to consider? Let me ask you this question. Are there any aspects of your environment that you share with your client?

Ali: That's difficult to tell as it's not possible, without a web cam to tell what it's like, where the client is.

Jethro: Well yes that's true but can you think of some aspects of the client that must be present for them and for you too?

Ali: Yes, the computers.

Jethro: Go one.

Ali: The keyboard, the monitor, desk, chair.

Jethro: Ok that's good. So perhaps you could consider these common shared aspects of the environment as possible elements for building rapport, you could make a reference to them in your emails and that could be your way of saying to your client that you have a common experience....

Let's look at these two texts...

I read your letter today and I was so immersed in what you wrote that I was almost late replying to you.

I read your letter on my monitor screen today and I was so immersed in reading what was on the screen before me that I was almost late in sitting down to the keyboard and replying

Man: I see that the second reply would show a common experience and could help build rapport.

Jethro: Yes it's something you could consider, but I wouldn't suggest you constantly refer to elements of your keyboard, monitor, desk , mouse etc, through the bulk of your email, but you may wish to use this option in the occasional email, at the start or end of a composition. It's really about you having the choice....

In our informal chat meeting last week, you were "meeting" each other for the first time. What sort of things were you discussing between yourselves?

Baz: I was discussing the terrible weather.

Man: I was discussing the fact that we cannot see each other.

Geraldine: I was discussing my experience as an online therapist with someone else.

Jethro: Thank you. So as you had never met before, you started to build rapport with each other by talking about your common shared experience. How would you have reacted if someone on the workshop said....?

"I spent all last night painting the door to my new ant farm".

Man: Not a good opener really LOL.

Ali: Unless you're at an ant farm convention LOL.

Jethro: Exactly! I'm not saying here that staying up late and painting the door to your ant farm is weird, as **all behaviour is acceptable in the right context** but in this instance it's not a great way of building rapport because on a workshop related to online therapy, it's unlikely to be a common shared experience....

So far we have been talking about rapport building possibilities, and every aspect of what we have currently discussed will work in asynchronous exchange as well as synchronous exchange. However there are some aspects to rapport building that only relate to synchronous exchange that is when using a chat format. Any ideas?

Ali: Well one thing that I am aware of in chat is that sometimes the client can take a long time to respond.

Jethro: Ok. That's good. So you could consider responding at the same rate as them?

Ali: Well I never have considered that.

Jethro: What does it feel like for you when you have to wait for their response?

Ali: It can feel frustrating sometimes.

Jethro: And could it be that your client may feel something too. If they take 30 seconds to create and send a message and you reply 2 seconds later?

Ali: I think if I took a long time to construct and send a line of text and then a reply came back 2 seconds later, I would feel that I was under pressure to respond quicker.

Jethro: Good. That's good feedback. So again, you may wish to think about this aspect of rapport building that really only applies to synchronous work...

There is of course something else here that I would also like to you keep in mind, and what I am going to say here may lead you to think that there is no point at all in building rapport online in the first place. We are in unexplored territory here...

It's well known that in online therapy, people will often "jump in" feet first and start talking about their issues, problems, and challenges, much quicker than they would in the face-to-face world. Anyone know what this is called?

Mark: Disinhibition.

Jethro: Yes it's the disinhibition effect, and it can lead to a client spilling out the most intimate details of what has happened in their life in the first email, or in the first few text exchanges. Sometimes this can be a bit overwhelming and it's caused by the fact that the client will perceive you as being totally anonymous. I recently got a FIRST email from a client that read something like this...

..im married and i have a lot of sex with prostitutes. i don't love them and i know that when im having sex with them they are just whores but they let me blow off my sexual energy when i cant do that with my wife who has turned into my mother in some ways..

Hag: Yes that's pretty dishinibiting.

Jethro: So for a first email, the client has lost a lot of his inhibitions. It's possible that this person may be like this with everyone he meets face-to-face, but it's unlikely that he would be like this with his first face-to-face meeting with a therapist. Once the client perceives that he or she is anonymous, then that anonymity can increase disinhibition. They are not connected directly to you and this separation from the real world allows them to open up more easily. Also the client and the therapist are invisible; if the client is constructing an email to you and it is 2 days before you are due to receive it, then in reality you are not really there, even when the client is constructing the email. That's not so for synchronous chat, but in email exchange you are not there when the email is being constructed, and that's got to be another big boost for the disinhibition effect, which is increased by this invisibility, and the delayed exchanges. So tell me anyone, what happens inside your head when you read this? I'm not so much interested in what you perceive about the client, but what happens inside **your** head when you read it...

Hello there I'm writing to let you know that this is my first attempt at using email as a way of communicating with a therapist.

Mark: Well when I read it, I read it inside my head and not out loud.

Jethro: And when you did that, whose voice did you hear inside your head.

Mark: Well now you mention it although I was reading the text of someone else, it was actually my own voice that I heard inside my head.

Jethro: So you used your own internal voice. I guess that you did that because you have no idea what the client sounds like. So, all the verbal construction in the communication between you and the client is all in your head. I had an experience where I was working online with a man, let's call him Paul Hapenfluger. He had a serious social phobia, and working online is a good way to start for someone with a social phobia as opposed to group therapy. Whilst I was working with him I started reading his email using my own voice but then I realised after a while that I had made up a voice for him. This voice was a timid, weak voice with little power. After about 10 email exchanges we ended and he had moved on enough to feel that he wanted to have face-to-face therapy and actually meet a therapist.

At the time I was working in a group practice and so I referred him on to a face-to-face therapist in my practice. One day I was in the practice reception area when a man by the name of Paul Hapenfluger walked in and spoke to the receptionist. He spoke with a strong regional accent and his voice could be described as full and deep with a great resonance, so very different from what I had interjected into my head...

Ali: perhaps all that online therapy changed his voice LOL.

Jethro: So when a client reads your emails it's likely that they would use their voice and not yours when they are reading it, as they probably do not know what you sound like. This aspect of online communication increases the perception that there is only one person in the therapy and therefore it's a factor that increases disinhibition....

When I work in a university setting doing face-to-face work I do not tend to wear a suit and a tie and I do that for a conscious reason. The reason I do it is because none of the students I see will be turning up to see me wearing suits and ties. So as a way of making the students feel that I am more like them, and as a way of using my environment to build rapport, I tend to wear casual clothes, a t-shirt and jeans perhaps. Can you imagine what the students might perceive if they turned up to see me and I was wearing a white coat over a suit?

Ali: Well I wouldn't feel comfortable because I would feel that you were about to give me a medical.

Jethro: Yes. And clothes and our appearance can send out a lot of messages about equality and inequality. It is less defined now, I know and I have seen some very wealthy people that spend a fortune on looking like they are homeless, but the way you look can have an impact on how inhibited people can feel when initially communicating. However, when working online, there are no visible trappings that may associate the therapist and the client with the cues of wealth, power or status. There is a great equalising effect online and that sense of equality will also lead to the client being less inhibited...

When you are working online you can consider matching the client's experiences in order to build rapport. Again, you will need to use your experience and integrity depending on what you want. Let me say that again. You will have to use your experience and integrity depending on WHAT YOU WANT...

So we have looked at building rapport online with a client and how different it is to building rapport in a face-to-face environment. A lot of what we have discussed is really still classed as in the realm of being suitable for experimentation, and as we are in a new theatre of work regarding online psychotherapy, there are many new exciting aspects of how you can consider and use all or any of the useful things we have raised here today, for your consideration....

Some people may be saying to themselves that there are no answers here, and at this point I could say that is true, but I do know of many times when I have been in the company of great teachers, when the learning has not come from the answers I was given but from the questions that I asked myself at the time. I often recall the confusion after a day working with great teachers, and now I realise that from that confusion came original thought and new behaviour. You can explore what we have looked at now and make this, your own.

Chapter 3.

Goal achievement.

Jethro: Welcome back...

A few years ago, I was talking to a man who had been seeing a therapist for about a year. He told me that his therapist was a wonderful person, a great listener, with lots of warmth and understanding. He told me that after he had seen her he would often feel great, and that he really looked forward to his weekly sessions. I asked him if he minded telling me why he went to see her in the first place. He was very open and rather proudly told me that he went to see her because he had a drink problem and was often violent to others when he was under the influence of alcohol. I asked him if he was still drinking heavily and violent. He replied that unfortunately he was still drinking and still violent to others but added that the counselling was going well....

I asked him if the counsellor had ever asked him what he wanted from therapy and his reply was...

" Er....well...er....no..."

So this person had been seeing a therapist, but had made no real behavioural changes relating to his drink problem...

Here's a model that you can work with that would favour an asynchronous approach, as you could send the tasks by an email attachment. Of course if you were working synchronously, you could still send the whole chunk as a file, but I would go for an attachment in an email as it's neater. If you were working in synchronous mode, you could just ask them to give you a response to each individual question...

Some people have a clear idea of what they want; others don't have a clear idea of what they want but are very clear **on what they don't want.**

If you openly ask a client in an email "What do you want", it may seem a little "full on" and may not be a great way to build rapport, so one way of getting someone to tell you what they want is by asking them to do this little exercise...

For example...

So John, I read over your initial email and thought that there was rather a lot there, in fact I did feel that I didn't quite know where to start as there seemed to be so many aspects of your life that you mentioned. I wonder if we could clarify the work we need to focus on.

John, I wonder if you could write down a series of lists under the following headings

A list of things you have in your life and you really want to keep (this is your "I'm grateful for" list). The items in these lists can be objects, people, aspects of your personality, in fact anything that comes into your head.

Also

A list of things you have in your life but you don't want.

And

A list of things you don't have in your life but you want.

And finally, and some say this is a little odd but it makes up the quartet.

A list of things you don't have in your life and you don't want (This is your "fear" list).

Perhaps John you could take some time to consider what would go under each list for you. As you have a week to reply, you make want to take some time to decide what you really want to add to your lists. There is no "right" or "wrong" and the length of the lists are up to you. **You can send me your list when you reply in your next email if you wish.**

John's Reply

Have and want to keep

House
Job
Car
Sense of humour
Close friend
Family

Have but don't want

Anxiety
Fear of going to parties
Shyness
Sweaty hands
Panic attacks

Don't have but want

Confidence
More friends
Jane who works next to me to like me more

Don't have and don't want

Cancer
Debt

Jethro: So in one email exchange, this technique will allow you to establish a blueprint for client goals. Now we can see what John wants and what he doesn't want...

Let's have a look at John's goals in a slightly different way now. When working with goals in a linguistic way, it's worth looking at whether a person's goal is **WELL FORMED.**

Has anyone here come across the term **well formed outcome** before...?

O.K, well when working online, it helps if the client can have a way of thinking and expressing an outcome in a way that makes them verifiable and also achievable.

Man: Like SMART goals.

Jethro: By smart, you mean goals that are...

Specific
Measurable
Achievable
Realistic
Timed

Man: Exactly.

Jethro: Well SMART only gives a partial picture, they can be helpful, but personally I feel that working with well-formed outcomes is a better way of working online. Here is a summary of well formed-ness in relation to outcomes. Let's have a look at them, and then we can go back and have a look at John's lists and see if he has any outcomes that might not be well formed. If they are not well formed then it could be that John may have a harder time achieving those goals that have been listed.

There are six main elements to having a well-formed outcome...

The goal should be stated positively.

For example

I want to do well

As opposed to

I don't want to do badly

The goal needs to be put into context.

For example

I want to have confidence when I am at parties with my friends

As opposed to

I want confidence

Also, the goal needs to be expressed in terms that let the person stating the goal, become aware of what they will see, hear and feel (and perhaps even smell and taste) when they have achieved the goal...

 I refer to this as having a sensory specific element to it.

For example...

When I have achieved my goal of having confidence at parties with my friends I will see myself smiling at people I want to talk to, approaching people to talk to, hearing my voice as I speak to them in a calm voice, and I will feel a sense of excitement. I will hear myself laughing and see others responding.

Jethro: **The goal has to have a great percentage of being fulfilled by the person wanting the goal...**

We can look at this in more detail in a moment, but if you have a greater chance of achieving a goal yourself, then it's more likely to happen than if others are involved greatly in your goal achievement...

The effects of achieving the goal have to be considered.

If you gain something, you will also loose something too. For instance, if you gain fame, you will lose anonymity. I know some people have focused too much on what it's like to achieve that goal, and not realised what they will lose. So it's certainly worth considering...

The goal has to be worthwhile for the person stating the goal.

A goal that isn't worthwhile will not be very motivating. If I have a goal of "I want to have the world's greatest postage stamp collection", then it just doesn't seem a worthwhile goal to me, and so it's unlikely to be a goal I will achieve. For someone else, it may be a different story...

So let's have a look at John's list again and explore how his lists relate to well formed outcomes...

Now for John, everything in his world would fit into one of those lists. This old sweater I am now wearing for instance.

Geraldine: Probably in the "don't have don't want" section perhaps? LOL.

Jethro: Well I guess it's all a matter of taste but I guess it is good that you cannot see it. LOL...

The two lists with the titles "have and want to keep" and "don't have and don't want" are really two lists that ideally do not need to change at all for John. If these stay this way then John will stay happy and they can be used to feed back to the client some aspects of their life that actually do not need to change.

Man: Why bother getting a client to list them in the first place?

Jethro: Well I agree, you don't have to use these two elements, but you can get some useful information from them that can be used in your emails to validate the client's experience and life. We know that John feels he has a sense of humour, that's useful information. It could alter the way you text or email John. Knowing he has listed himself as having a sense of humour could give you leverage for rapport and change.

Here's Johns list of what he "has and doesn't want" as well as his "don't have but want" list. If you look at these two lists and our rules regarding well-formed outcomes, can you see any aspects of his lists that are not well formed?

Have but don't want

Anxiety
Fear of going to parties
Shyness
Sweaty hands
Panic attacks

Don't have but want

Confidence
More friends
Jane who works next to me to like me more

Man: Well the whole section of "have and don't want" is not well formed as all those items are stated in the negative.

Jethro: How do you mean?

Man: John is stating what he doesn't wasn't and that's very negative.

Jethro: Yes, exactly. Some people are very good at listing what they don't want and as a consequence they can come up with a lot of goals that are just not well formed. When that happens, you can ask your client to reframe that section of the lists to make them positive.

For instance...

John, I noticed that you have listed five items in your "have but don't want" list. I wonder if you could take a look at them and reframe them so that you could change them to things that you **want instead**. For example, if a person has sadness, then they don't have happiness. If a person has debt, then they don't have solvency.

Could you have a look at those items on your list and email me what you want instead?

Jethro: Often they can be the opposite of what you have...

John's reply list.

Have but don't want

Anxiety
Fear of going to parties
Shyness
Sweaty hands
Panic attacks

Want instead
To focus on the here and now
Confidence when going to parties
Confidence
To be able to focus on things around me
Calm feelings

Jethro: OK, any others that might not be well formed?

Man: The one listed as "Jane who works next to me, to like me more" - It's in the "don't have but want" list.

Jethro: Yes I agree, that's not well formed because it's not about him at all; it's all about Jane.

Ali: Can you explain that one again?

Jethro: Yes of course, here's another example. If I want to take off my sweater then that's a well formed outcome for me as I have a good chance of being able to do that myself...

If my goal was to get you to take off my sweater, then that wouldn't be well formed because I wouldn't have a good chance of being able to do that myself. If you don't want to take my sweater off and my goal is for you to take it off for me, then my sweater isn't going to be taken off. Does that make sense?

Ali: Yes it does.

Jethro: So perhaps John could reframe that statement too, so that it was well formed. For example...

I would like to get on better with Jane when I am at work with her...

That would be one way of looking at it. At least this way he's in control of his outcome more than before.

And what can we read about the context of John's goals? Well as he has only made a short-list, he's not really contextualised many of them. He has referred to "getting on with Jane whilst he is at work" so that has some contextualisation. He lists...

Confidence

More friends

So here you could reply to him either via an email exchange or by text, the latter being much more immediate and responsive for this way of working.

In an email you may wish to write...

John, I noticed that you said you wanted to have confidence and more friends, and I'm guessing that one is linked to the other for you. If you had more confidence, you would feel as if you could have more friends. I wonder if you could consider the following

Where and when exactly would you like to have confidence?

Jethro: Of course if you were working in chat, you may feel the need to be more immediate in your response as it may take you too long to type a long paragraph.

Man: Yes I agree, I find that when I'm using chat, both my clients and myself tend to use much shorter lines of communication when sending the information.

Jethro: And that's a good reason why you will probably be able to be more direct in a chat format, without breaking any rapport, as BOTH OF YOU will be doing the same thing...

And also to make it sensory specific for John...

In Email...

..And could you tell me John what would it be like for you when you have achieved your goal on your list and you have confidence in those areas? Could you write back and let me know what you will specifically be doing differently. How will you be behaving differently? What will John see? What will John hear? How will he feel?

And in Chat...

And what will your see, hear and feel when you have achieved your goal?

Jethro: So lets backtrack a moment. If you are going to have online exchange with a client, then it will help you and the client if you can establish some goals for therapy. The benefit being that you can establish whether the therapy is working. It can allow the client and the therapist to revisit the goals and see what's working and what needs to be worked on. This method of using lists is one way of doing that. I personally believe that this method can work well when working in an asynchronous way as well as with synchronous work. In asynchronous work there is that **zone of reflection** where there is a period of time, where the client and the therapist can reflect on the response. Of course this is a big difference between asynchronous and synchronous work. If we were going to elicit a client's outcome for therapy in a synchronous setting how would we approach it...?

Ali: I think you could be more direct and ask them what they wanted from therapy.

Jethro: Well yes, I'm sure that could work but remember that a lot of people are very good at knowing what they don't want.

Ali: Ok I think I could bear this model in mind and use it in a more flexible way.

Jethro: Well let's have a look at how the model could come up in a synchronous chat.

John: I guess I've never been happy with any events that involve people

Jethro: So I hear you say that you are not happy around people, is that all people?

John: Well I'm fine with a few close friends but it's when I have to go to parties or meet new groups at work.

Jethro: John, so I hear that you have a few close friends now, so I assume that you have been able to make friends in the past

John: Well yes, I never thought of that but its really parties and meetings that freak me out

Jethro: So John what do you want get out of working here specifically in connection with what we are discussing now?

John: Well I want people to be able to instantly like me

Jethro: **Note: this is not a well-formed outcome.**

Jethro: John, that would be nice and I think that is something that I could see as an amazing thing...

but I wonder how realistic it is...

When you say you would like people to instantly like you...

 It sounds as if that's not under your control.

John: True, I agree with that.

Jethro: How could you phrase it so that you had control over your actions or emotions?

John: Erm.... I would like to be able to feel confident and behave in a confident way when I am meeting strangers for the first time.

Jethro: And how will you know when you have achieved that goal?

John: I will be looking at them directly, being curious about them. I will be shaking hands with new people.

Jethro: Can you see that now?

John: Yes actually.

Jethro: What's that like?

John: Oddly enough it feels like good.

Mark: I noticed that you used dots .... When you were typing.

Jethro: Yes, I tend to use this when working synchronously. It allows me to pace my sentences and send them in small chunks to the client, without the client responding. Is that concept new to you Mark?

Mark: Yes it is but now I'm aware that we have been working that way on the course too LOL.

Jethro: Sometimes people may be familiar with this way of chat exchange, using dots as a way of saying "I'm talking so don't interrupt me yet". If not, you may wish to explain that you like to send in small chunks when you are writing to them and when they see the dots.... it means that you are still typing, and so they can wait until your full stop before they get their turn to respond.

Geraldine: And that way it seems more conversational too.

Jethro: Yes, and when working synchronously there is a great danger, from a communication point of view to generate two threads of conversation at the same time, or even more. This can be very confusing for both participants and using dots is a good way of preventing this happening.

Hag: Any chance of an example of what could go wrong ☹

Jethro: OK here's an example...

Client: So I went to the store and he was there, smirking as he walked down the aisles.

Therapist: And so he was there, waiting for you.

Client: He had a race the next day and he was buying stuff for his bike. I hate it when he races.

Therapist: So what sort of racing is it, is it something that could be dangerous for him?

Client: He was buying oil I think.

Therapist: Oh at the store?

Client: Yes, he drives a huge motorbike.

Jethro: As soon as you experience this, then you need to instruct the client that two threads have been created and that you need to focus on just one. Using dots to say that you are still "talking" helps....

If, when you are working synchronously and there is a miscommunication, or the start of something confusing, it's best to **STOP** and go for clarity; otherwise you may continue to be synchronously confused...

One other way of setting up a synchronous session is to get the client to send an **introductory email** to you so that you will have an idea what they would like to talk about when working synchronously. This can allow you to do some pre-reading or pre-work on what they want to explore so that you are well versed in what they want to discover or change before the synchronous session starts.

Man: And I guess that means that the therapist gets fewer surprises.

Jethro: Also when you are working synchronously, its worthwhile to let your client know that you will probably both be making typing errors as you text each other. This is due to the spontaneous nature of working this way.

Here's an example...

Jethro: John, as it's our first meeting here today there's one more thing I would like to say before we start. May I continue?

John: Sure

Jethro: Well as we are using chat, we may make some typing erors alang the way. **I already have done** ☺ If that hapens, then I want to say that it's ok, if either of us do so. There's no need to apologise or to correct a typing error, unless either of us feels that it really seems confusimng. How are you with that?

John: Yes Im fine with that. I was worried about my spelling because when I type fast I do make silly mistajkes so Im glad we spoke about this already

Jethro: So if you keep the concept of the outcome model on the back burner when you are working synchronously, you can allow it to be a mental aid for you so that you can help the client get what they want...

Any questions....

Baz: So you could have a blank sheet with a full explanation on how to fill it in, and send it to a client as part of their homework?

Jethro: Yes, that's a great way of doing it provided there is an explanation of what they are expected to do that goes with it.

Chapter 4.

More goals online.

Jethro: I have already mentioned that behavioural change is one aspect of what we can look for, and one question that I often ask when working synchronously, although you can also add it to the end of an email is this question...

As a result of our work today, what do you think you will <u>do</u> differently from now on?

Jethro: Or if it's in an email...

John, I have written a lot in my response today. I'm sure that you will have a lot to think about. As you read over what I have written, you may think how it relates to you. As you do that, I wonder if you could consider this question.

What do you think you will <u>do</u> differently as a result of our last two email exchanges?

Jethro: So when working synchronously or asynchronously, you and your client could utilise the concept of having goals for therapy, in order that you can see what your client wants to achieve. You can then check whether it's a valid goal, or well formed, and use feedback to determine how the work you are doing together is effective in allowing the client to achieve those goals...

So I would like you to consider the importance of working with your client to determine what they want to get out of therapy and how you could use some of these skills to help you achieve that goal. Once you have discovered the template of what the client feels they need to change, you can use the concept of well-formed outcomes to allow the client and the therapist to know where to focus, as well as to follow whether the client is achieving their goals...

Often a client will present a problem in a written format that will indicate that a specific action will lead to a specific event. It's a cause effect that has no choice in its concept.

Mark: So, it's a "this causes that" we have already discussed in our earlier work.

Jethro: Yes, I'm glad you remembered. Thank you. The cause effect has a limitation that presupposes that the cause will certainly lead to the effect. As therapists working online we need to look at how we can build in "choice" to the concept so that the client will be able to look at other options...

I would also like you to consider the following model with regards to the "this means that", or complex equivalence...

Probably the best way to explain this is to look at an example...

Can anyone give me an example of a "this causes that", or a "this means that"?

Ali: If I become depressed, he will leave me.

Jethro: Thanks, so the sentence shows **one option.**

Becoming depressed = he will leave her.

I would like you to consider the following that could apply too...

Becoming depressed = he will NOT leave her.

NOT becoming depressed = he will leave her.

NOT becoming depressed = he will NOT leave her.

Ali: So you are then able to indicate to a client that what was initially perceived a one way, no choice, and no option for the client, could actually have four options.

Jethro: Yes.

Baz: That's an interesting way of allowing the client to explore new ways and new choices. I hadn't seen it like that before and it's so easy to consider.

Jethro: Shall we have another one?

If I tell my wife I am having an affair she **WILL** leave me.

If I tell my wife I am having an affair she **WON'T** leave me.

If **I DON'T** tell my wife I am having an affair she **WILL** leave me.

If **I DON'T** tell my wife I am having an affair she **WON'T** leave me...

Let's have a look at the logic behind this for a moment. One way of looking at it is to keep the following questions in your head...

 1) What would happen if you did?

 2) What would happen if you didn't?

3) What wouldn't happen if you did?

4) What wouldn't happen if you didn't...?

We can use this formula when working with synchronously, by the direct intervention of asking each question one at a time...

Client: I know that if I tell my parents I am pregnant, they will throw me out.

Therapist: So you are saying that if you don't tell then, they will not throw you out?

Client: Yes.

Therapist: Could it be the case that even if you do not tell your parents you are pregnant they will still ask you to leave the house?

Client: I don't think so. I am safe now that they do not know I am pregnant. Although, my parents would often threaten to throw me out of the house, whenever I was naughty.

Therapist: So you have had experiences in the past when things have been bad for you and your parents, and even though they have threatened to throw you out, they never did?

Client: Yes, I guess so but this would be the worst ever.

Therapist: But could it be that you are making an assumption, and that it could be possible that if you tell your parents, they may get angry, shout and threaten to throw you out but not actually carry it through?

Mark: I see that the questions are allowing the client to think about options, even if in some cases the client may reject them.

Geraldine: I found that the options made a "shift" for me in my head when I read them.

Jethro: That's an interesting response, and perhaps that's why the use of this type of model in working online can be helpful for the client too...

Also, the model can be expanded to allow the client to consider more variations. So far, we have only explored two factors, let's call them A and B, but the model can be expanded to include added factors, let's call them factors C and D in the example below. By using the added factors, the client can then consider even more options and their outcomes...

Factor A = Tell my parents I'm pregnant.

Factor B = Parents throw me out.

Factor C = Get job.
.
Factor D = Don't get job.

Now the therapist can ask the client more questions relating to their new choices...

What would happen if you did A, B and C.

What would happen if you didn't do A and B but did C etc...

Hag: I am thinking of a client who often has several issues and we only focus on how the issue will impact on one aspect of their life. I see this model as a way of getting the client to have a look at how the issue can impact on other parts of their life, perhaps even in a positive way.

Baz: Can it work when using email exchange too?

Jethro: Well yes I think so, here's an example from a therapist using the above method in an email...

I read in your last email that you said that you were concerned that all the extra time you were spending on your degree studies would mean that your boyfriend would be unfaithful to you.

You may wish to look at the above options and make some comments under the headings below.

What will happen to your relationship if you continue your degree?

What won't happen to your relationship if you continue your degree?

What will happen to your relationship if you don't continue your degree?

What won't happen to your relationship if you don't continue your degree?

Alice, you may wish to have a look at those questions and give me some feedback for next time

Jethro: The response by the client...

What will happen to your relationship if you continue your degree?

I think that John may get bored with being alone and he will decide to leave me.

What won't happen to your relationship if you continue your degree?

John and I won't be able to spend the next 12 weeks together every evening

What will happen to your relationship if you don't continue your degree?

I will get to spend every night with John for the next 12 weeks

What won't happen to your relationship if you don't continue your degree?

It won't end

Man: On reading what the client Alice wrote, I could see that this would allow me to open up the discussion if I were to reply to her.

Jethro: Can you expand on that?

Man: Well I was thinking about asking Alice about the evidence that would support her comments. I am thinking about asking Alice if there has ever been a previous occasion where he was bored because she had to work. I'm also thinking about whether there is any evidence that he has left her before and returned. I'm thinking about this response by Alice...

John and I won't be able to spend the next 12 weeks together every evening.

Man: Here I'm thinking about the fact that she used the term "12 weeks" and if that is the remainder of her degree study time, then I could assume that she has done at least 2 years of the degree already and he hasn't left. I wonder what's different about the last 12 weeks.

Ali: That jumped out at me too, it's only 12 weeks out of a degree of three years.

I will get to spend every night with John for the next 12 weeks.

Man: Here I was thinking about John. Would he really be happy to spend every night with Alice for the next 12 weeks? Perhaps he may want to end the relationship if she did!

Ali: And the last one.

Man: Yes I pondered on that and realised that Alice was totally looking at how 1 affects 2 and not how it affects 3 and 4 etc.

What won't happen to your relationship if you don't continue your degree?

It won't end.

Yes Alice but what other things won't happen because you have ended your degree?

Man: By this question I am thinking about how Alice can consider how ending her degree can impact on other things, these may or may not be related to John. Her future career, a house, car, could all be 3, 4, and 5.

Geraldine: I think that as a therapist I would often ask these sorts of questions, but it's good to have a model to fallback on and know that it's a good way of expanding thinking and options for the client in an exercise via email.

Ali: And in future emails, what would you do if a client made a comment about their listed goals?

Jethro: I think it's important to utilise as much as is said to you by the client, if you have time to respond. If a client states that they have made some headway, then I feel that it's important to recognise that in the response.

Ali: And if they were frustrated because they stated that they were not achieving the goal would you then see that as "information", so that you could then look at other options?

Man: I think that such a comment from a client would be great feedback and not failure on their part. They have shown that they are aware of the fact that they have not achieved their goal yet, and now the therapist can explore any flexibility that could be added to the client's strategy.

Jethro: Thank you, a good point Man...

So you may wish to keep this model in your head, or on your desk, so that if you want to explore the client's perceived limitations, you can hopefully allow them to consider new options that they may not have considered.

Chapter 5.

Asking questions online.

Jethro: So now let's move on from looking at what a person wants from therapy and ways of exploring, checking and working with their outcomes, to something else...

Now we are going deeper into text to see if we can use questions to gather more information about the client's model of the world, to expand any limitations they may perceive they have, and to see if we can start the process of changing the meaning of the client's world, particularly if that meaning is having negative impact on them. All these aspects can be seen in the text body itself and this session will hopefully go a long way in allowing you to learn new ways to recognise certain language patterns and, more importantly, how to respond to them...

Once again, we will be looking at this from a synchronous and an asynchronous perspective. The things that you will learn now will allow you to become even more skilled at what you do...

As we are working as online therapists, we are primarily concerned with how thoughts are translated into words. Our clients are using words to describe their experiences. The first thing to note here is that the text is not the experience itself. You need to consider, that before the text is written, there is initially the experience itself, and then after that, there is a person's representation of that experience, and finally there is the generation of that client's representation of that experience in text...

Man: It's like Chinese whispers.

Jethro: Yes, that's a good analogy. First there is the experience – then a slightly altered view of that comes about when a person makes sense of that experience, and then a further alteration when a client puts down that experience in text...

When my son was a small child we went for a walk to the park. On the way he saw a BMW car and said to me, "Dad, what's that?" I told him it was a car. A few seconds later another car, an Audi, went past and he said "Dad what's that?" I told him again it was another car. He looked confused at this point and said "But how can they both be cars?" After a chat with him I realised that he wasn't able to generalise that BMW and Audi were both types of car. Of course now he's older he can generalise that difference...

Imagine what it would be like for adults if they couldn't generalise their learning. I have modern minimalist style chromium doorknobs in my house and yet my friend has antique Victorian brass doorknobs in his house. Imagine if I couldn't generalise that they are both types of doorknob? If that was the case I could find myself stuck behind quite a few doors...!

So we know that generalising is something that can be part of our experience, and of course that can be expressed in text by our clients...

In these cases however, they are using generalisations to create a world that they are not happy with...

Here are a few generalisations...

Nobody loves me
My partner never does the washing up
All men are bastards

Jethro: So with generalisations there are elements, or pieces of a person's original experience, that have come to represent the entire category of which the experience is an example. As therapists, we can ask questions that allow the client to look at those generalisations and then, as they reply, they can start the process where they expand on their model of the world...

For example...

> Client: I can never do anything right.
>
> Therapist: can you think of a time when you did something right?
>
> Client: Nothing happens to me.
>
> Therapist: Can you think of a time when something happened to you?

Jethro: And with those examples above, perhaps you can see how valuable this can be in synchronous work.

Man: Yes. It's focused and has immediacy to it.

Hag: So how would you respond in an email?

Jethro: Very much the same, but you could arrange your question in the form of a paragraph or a few sentences...

Let's have a look at a piece of text...

> Client: I have always been the one that has to do everything at work.

Therapist's response...

> Therapist: I noticed in your last email that you said that you were always being the one having to do everything. When I saw those words I wondered how true that was. I wonder if you have **always** been the one. If that's the case I wonder who did those things before you started. Also I wonder if you really have to do **everything** at work.

Jethro: Sometimes the questions that you use as a response can be used in a humorous way and of course humour can have an important place in therapy...

Client: I do everything at work.

Therapist: Wow! Perhaps you could get all the others made redundant and give your self a pay rise. The company would make some significant salary savings with all the other staff laid off. Do you really do **everything?**

Client: No but sometimes it just feels that way.

Therapist: So could it be that what you feel may not actually be realistic?

Client: Yes I guess I tend to make things a lot worse than they actually are.

Therapist: And I wonder if the "everything" word that you typed is part of your thinking?

Client: Yes I do that all the time.

Therapist: **All** the time?

Client: That's funny, yes I don't do it all the time but I do it an awful lot.

Therapist: Can you feel the difference between "all the time" and "a lot?"

Client: Yes, "all the time" seems so much more debilitating for me than "a lot".

Therapist: And could the same apply to when you use "everything"

Client: Yes it does.

Jethro: Ok so I hope you all agree that being aware of generalisations in emails and text exchanges, and then responding to them is one way of getting the client to explore their world and then start the process of making changes...

Shall we examine another?
Geraldine: Yes please.

Jethro: Let's imagine a text or a section in an email where a client wrote this...

I can't live without him.

Jethro: What response would you consider?

Mark: If you feel you can't live without him, how does that make you feel?

Ali: It sounds as if you are stuck in your life at the moment.

Jethro: Yes, I can understand those responses and I can see that they are good ways of building empathic rapport with a client; however I would like you to consider these two responses...

What stops you from being able to live without him?

What would happen if you did live without him?

Jethro: What comes to mind when you see the questions I have posed?

Man: Well they seem to have a sort of propulsion to them.

Ali: They are more about moving the client on than empathic questions.

Jethro: So, if it were synchronous work...

I just can't live without him.

What stops you?

I don't have the emotional strength or the finances.

Jethro: Before I continue, I would like to mention here that the question, "what stops you" has a tendency to keep the client in the "problem space", because they will invariably give you lots of information as to why they are stuck. However, this can be very useful for both the therapist and the client, because it allows the client to express their limitations. Now that the client has responded this way, the therapist does not have to guess why the client is stuck. The cards are on the table. In the case above, the therapist can now focus on the "emotional strength", whatever that means, and the financial aspects of the text exchange...

What if I asked....?

Q: I just can't live without him

R: What would happen if you did?

Ali: Well I can see straight away that this question takes the client to the solution space. I like that very much.

Jethro: Yes, and remember it's always worth considering that you can "soften" these questions with opening lines such as...

I noticed that you said that you can't live without him and I'm wondering what you believe would happen if you did?

And the client's response...

Q: What would happen if you did?

R: Well if I left him I would have to get a job and earn my own money.

Jethro: Here's another for you...

I won't pass my English exam.

Baz: what stops you?
Ali: What would happen if you did?

Jethro: I guess you have got it. You can use those questions in emails too, but you might need to nest the questions around other text to make the response softer...

Jane, I read that you said that you couldn't leave your partner and I was asking myself when I read that, just exactly what is going on for you that stops you from leaving her?

Perhaps you could think about that over the next few days and get back to me after you have had time to consider just exactly what is stopping you from leaving her?

Baz: What is the name given to these patterns?

Jethro: I'm glad you asked, but you might not be so happy when I tell you what they are called. In fact they are called modal operators of possibility, well you did ask. I sometimes refer to them as "can't do's", they cover a whole load of other text expressions too such as...

Won't, cant, may not, impossible...

Also to make things even more interesting, there is a similar linguistic pattern called a modal operator of necessity, this is similar, but relates to words like should, must, need to etc. Again I personally refer to these as "must do's", but being able to remember the term modal operator or being able to determine whether the expression is a modal operator of necessity or of possibility at this stage is not that important. If you want to do that, then its fine, but the main thing is that you recognise the following types of text and have a way of responding to them...

I must get home for dinner
You should feel guilty
I can't understand what you mean

I couldn't refuse her

All the above can have a response...

What would happen if you did?
What would happen if you didn't?

The questions are a great way of uncovering the effects of a solution, or what the consequences will be if the person stays in the problem.

Let's go further shall we...?

I want you to consider examples of **deletions...**

Quite recently I had an email from a client and she said that her parents hurt her a lot when she was little....

So when I say to you now "my parents hurt me", what does that conjure up for you?

Mark: I made a picture of a man twisting a little girl's arm.

Ali: I saw a man shouting very loud in the face of a little girl.

Hag: I saw a man locking a little girl in her room and heard her sobbing.

Jethro: Wow, you do have great imaginations! So when you read that sentence, you were able to generate a whole range of sounds and images that went with the sentence....

So I hope that you can see that the sentence itself has generated a sort of vagueness around the word "hurt"...

In the sentence the verb "to hurt" is unspecified as to what the context of the "hurting" is. **This is called an unspecified verb**. If you have your linguistic head on when working, then you may want to notice these unspecified verbs and check them out.

In synchronous work...

When I was a teenager, my uncle helped me a lot.

How specifically did he help you?

Well he paid money into my bank account so I could continue my studies.

Jethro: In asynchronous...

My parents punish me when I get home. Afterwards I feel so bad that I just have to go into my room and cry. It's then when I feel like I want to hurt myself.

Jen, I wonder what it is that your parents do when they **punish** you that makes you feel so bad afterwards? What actually happens for you to feel bad......?

.. And when you are in your room and say you want to **hurt** yourself, what is it that you think about doing?

Jethro: In the above example we are attempting to uncover what the client means by "punish "and "hurt"...

Any questions or comments?

Baz: This is so very simple, and yet I can see that it can be a powerful way of gathering more information and making clear the client's words.

Jethro: As we are now looking specifically at sentences in text, let's go on....

Hers a typical email snippet...

Of course as time went by, I realised that my younger sister was better. After many years of not talking to each other, we met up at a funeral and I felt that the meeting went badly. I don't think we will meet up ever again

Man: Ever again?

Jethro: Er...well yes I'm so glad that you noticed that there was a generalisation in that sentence. It was my accidental deliberate mistake but well done for spotting the generalisation there. You have in fact raised a good point too. Your client may often use a whole range of language patterns in emails, and so a therapist will have to learn where to go with the response. For me, I tend to look at the area of the email where I feel that the meaning is not clear, or that by making it clearer to the client it will make the most difference to them. In this case, it may be that you would focus on the generalisation, but this was not another example of generalisations that I was considering, but an example of **comparisons...**

I realised that my younger sister was better.

And I felt that the meeting went badly.

Jethro: In these two examples, the client has given you two examples of missing information. In both cases a comparison is made, but it is not clear just exactly what the comparison is that is being referred to. **The comparison has been deleted...**

I realised that my younger sister was better.

Than me at talking to strangers
Than my brother

And I felt that the meeting went badly.

Compared to the last time we met
Compared to meeting I have with others in the family

Jethro: The way to respond to such comparisons is to ask...
"What are you comparing it to?"

So if we were working synchronously...

Client: My boss told me that the report had to be better.

Therapist: Better than what?

Client: Well I don't know actually but I do know that I felt awful when he told me.

Therapist: So you knew that your boss wanted the report to be better but you didn't know how it had to be better.

Client: Well no I didn't, I assumed that the entire report was rubbish.

Therapist: So I wonder if you asked him "how "it needed to be better, how that would affect you?

Client: I like it!! I will ask him that and then I will know exactly what I need to do. At the moment I'm imagining all sorts of ways to make it better and yet I do not really know.

Jethro: So look out for words like...

Good, better, worse, more, less, most, least, worse, worst

And the general theme of your response is...

"Compared to whom?"
"Compared to what?"

Mark: I see how these questions and responses can allow the client to access the limitations they believe they have.

Geraldine: I have found what has been said today so far very interesting. I work using synchronous text a lot, and many of my clients use the types of language patterns we have discussed.

Jethro: Have a look at this text...

This morning I woke up at 6:13 a.m. I opened my left eye 2 seconds before I opened my right eye and I looked up at the top right hand corner of the bedroom. I saw a small housefly 4 inches below the right hand corner. I moved my left hand from under the yellow silk covers and let my right hand move out from under the covers into the air outside the bed where I became aware that the temperature outside the bed was approx 20 degrees. At this point I made a picture in my head of my diary and this made form an image of a friend of mine in my head. I remembered that I had to meet my friend at 09:00 hrs at the corner of High Road and Acacia Road. I moved my right leg out of the bed and then my left leg. As I did so I heard the fly buzzing and as I looked up to the top right corner I noticed it had gone. As I scanned my head around the room I saw the fly had landed on the second windowpane on the bedroom window. I took 8 paces to the window, making another colour image in my head of my friend, and saying to myself "I have to let that fly out before I leave". I used my right hand to pull down on the white metal window latch and as I did so I noticed I could hear the sound of a nearby motorbike. I also noticed that the temperature outside the window was cooler than inside the bedroom. I would guess that outside it was approx 15 degrees. I moved my left hand in a left to right motion, approx two feet above the fly and as I did so it flew at an angle of 45 degrees towards the open window and then it flew out.

Or...

I got up this morning and let a fly out of my bedroom before I went out to meet a friend.

Jethro: Comments please.

Mark: Well I was switching right off as I read the first section; there is just too much information in the writing. It's too accurate.

Man: Technically there is nothing really wrong with it but there is so much useless information, it just leads to overload.

Jethro: And the second line?

Man: That just about says what happened in the first line, but I guess so much has been taken out of the experience that there are a lot of gaps now. Even so, I would rather read the second one. The first one would make for a horrendous novel.

Jethro: So the second line has had a lot of information deleted from it in order for the reader to remain interested in what is written. When you are reading an email from a client, you may come across areas where chunks of data may be deleted. Now as a therapist, sometimes uncovering those deletions can be another good way of gathering information.

Here are some examples of deletions and how you would respond to them to uncover the deleted section.

I am unhappy

About what?

By what?

They won't listen to me

Who wont?

She is a stronger acrobat

Stronger than whom?

Compared to whom?

He said my brother was stupid

Who said your brother was stupid?

All the above questions recover the missing deleted section. This form of logical questioning can allow the therapist to gather further information about the client experience. This can then allow the client to look differently at what is being expressed.

Ali: One cannot work with it unless one can fully be aware of what it is out there.

Jethro: Yes, that's right. Uncover it before working with it...

Again, I have come across these deletions more so in synchronous work than in email. I believe that deletions are more prone to happen when there is a greater sense of immediacy in the conversation. When a person is constructing an email, the need to respond in real time is reduced, and the client and the therapist can read over what they have written, correct spelling mistakes and check for grammar. In synchronous work, that real time experience leads to an increase in the number of deletions.

So without remembering the names of the deletions have a look at these statements and respond to uncover the deletions...

It's easy.

Man: What is easy?

They don't care about me.

Mark: Who doesn't care about you?

I am bored.

Geraldine: What are you bored with?

She destroyed him.

Hag: How did she destroy him?

You need to talk less.

Ali: I need to talk less than whom?

Jethro: Yes, you have got the main gist of how to respond to these deleted statements. Remember, they are not, in themselves a problem, because giving too much information can lead to problems too, but sometimes a deletion will require uncovering in order to recover any missing information. If you don't uncover the missing information you could end up in collusion where both the client and the therapist get lost in deletion land...

Client: I know that it hurts me so much when I'm not with him.

Therapist: Yes I can see how you must hurt that way.

Client: And then he comes along and suddenly it's worse.

Therapist: So it's worse when you are with him and worse when you are without him.

Client: No it's worse when I'm with John but better when I'm with Tariq.

Therapist: Oh so you are talking about two different people here..?

Jethro: Yes I know I might be insulting your intelligence with that example, but it's just an over the top way of showing you that if deletions are not uncovered then there can be a communication problem later.

Geraldine: And I can see that if I was the therapist and I had said, "It hurts when you are not with whom", that would have gotten the name of the person, and then asking "and then who comes along", would have clarified that two people are in the frame here.

Man: And you could ask "and suddenly its worse that what", and she could have responded that it was worse than when she was with Tariq, so that question too would have uncovered the deletion.

Jethro: So let's have a look at this example...

Communication with the club members is a terrible. Once there was discipline and now there is only chaos and frustration. I have spoken to Charles, the club president and told him that there is no respect at the club anymore. The process of what the club is doing has become a farce. The jealousy surrounding the summer competition has led to a great deal of hatred and I for one, feel that any connection I had with the old club has become a disaster. The club needs success but the club has failure and Charles needs to get an education in what's happening before I end, what has seemed like a marriage to this club for 40 years.

Man: I can't quite put my finger on it but the whole paragraph seems weird but really I cannot see why.

Jethro: Ok we'll take a look at some of the sentences. You may get an email from a client that has aspects of what is written here and I want to point this out to you so you can recognise what is going on, and how it may impact on the client. Of course I will also show you how to respond too. Let's break down some of this paragraph shall we?

Communication with the club members is terrible.

Compare that with

Communicating with the club members is terrible.

Geraldine: Well the first sentence that uses the word communication seems worse in some respect that the second sentence that uses the word communication but I'm not sure why.

Jethro: Yes, yes, I agree and you're getting there. Allow me to explain a little further...

In the above example, the word communication, is a variance on the word communicated, it has been **nominalised...**

Nominalised words can give the impression that what the client is referring to, is in some way **stuck and permanent**. I like to think that one of our roles is to make such stuckness become unstuck. This can be done by...

Recognising the word that has become nominalised.

Feeding the word back to the client in a denominalised form.

A nominalisation is when a verb appears as a noun. Once the verb has been converted into a noun it gives the impression that it is fixed, stuck and on going. Converting the nominalisation back to its denominalised form, allows the client to feel that stuckness is now unstuck...

Now the paragraph I illustrated contains a lot of nominalisations. There is nothing semantically incorrect with what has been written but as it has many nominalisations in its text body, it will give the reader the impression of vagueness, stuckness, and that there is an ongoing process to the main bulk of the written text as well as the client experience.

Man: For the client and the therapist too.

Jethro: Yes that's right, so let's have another look at that paragraph with the nominalisations highlighted...

<u>Communication</u> with the club members is a terrible. Once there was <u>discipline</u> and now there is only <u>chaos</u> and <u>frustration</u>. I have spoken to Charles, the club president and told him that there is no <u>respect</u> at the club anymore. The <u>process</u> of what the club is doing has become a <u>farce</u>. The <u>jealousy</u> surrounding the summer <u>competition</u> has led to a great deal of <u>hatred</u> and I for one, feel that any <u>connection</u> I had with the old club has become a <u>disaster</u>. The club had <u>success</u> but now the club has <u>failure</u> and Charles has to get an <u>education</u> in what's happening before I end what has seemed like a <u>marriage</u> to this club for 40 years.

 Jethro: One of the problems that a therapist can have when working with nominalisations is, in fact, **recognising** them. Here is a little tip to help you. As I have said, nominalisations are words that indicate some type of stuckness, so if you have a word that is a nominalisation it will appear semantically correct when put **after** this line…

"I am stuck with this………."

Let me explain further with an example of the nominalisation entitled "communication".

I am stuck with this communication.

Baz: Well that sounds ok to me from a linguistic point of view.

Jethro: Let's have a look at the denominalised form…

I am stuck with this communicating…

As you can see, the denominalised form **does not make a lot of sense** when added to the sentence.

Let's go back to the paragraph again and show all the nominalisations this way.

I'm stuck with this communication

I'm stuck with this discipline

I'm stuck with this chaos

I'm stuck with this frustration

I'm stuck with this respect

I'm stuck with this process

I'm stuck with this farce

I'm stuck with this jealousy

I'm stuck with this competition

I'm stuck with this connection

I'm stuck with this disaster

I'm stuck with this success

In stuck with this failure

I'm stuck with this education

I'm stuck with this marriage

As you can see, as these are all nominalisations, they make sense when added onto the end of the "I'm stuck with this..." line.

Let's denominalise them and see how nonsensical they become from a linguistic point of view.

I'm stuck with this communicating

I'm stuck with this disciplined

I'm stuck with this chaotic

I'm stuck with this frustrated

I'm stuck with this respecting

I'm stuck with this processed

I'm stuck with this farcical

I'm stuck with this jealous

I'm stuck with this competed

I'm stuck with this connected

In stuck with this disastrous

I'm stuck with this successful

I'm stuck with this failed

I'm stuck with this educated

I'm stuck with this married

Jethro: So now you can see that the denominalised forms do not make good linguistic sense.

Baz: Can you recap please; I'm almost at the hair pulling stage with this one.

Jethro: O.K, a nominalisation is usually a verb that has been turned into a noun...

Nominalisations give the writer and reader a sense of permanence and stuckness...

One way of testing a nominalisation is to use the line "I'm stuck with this....." before the suspect nominalisation...

And if the word **IS** a nominalisation, **IT WILL MAKE GRAMMATICAL SENSE...**

Once you have recognised it as a nominalisation, you can denominalise it so that the word is no longer perceived as permanent and unchangeable...

So if you were working with chat, here's an example...

Well my husband tries so hard but it's obvious that he does not have an education.

Jethro: The suspected nominalisation here is education...

I'm stuck with this education...makes sense so the word **is** a nominalisation.

The denominalised form is educated...

I'm stuck with this educated...does not make sense so that is the denominalised form...

Therapist's response could be...

In what way do you feel that your husband is not educated?

Let's do one more shall we?

Client: I thought that my marriage would lead me to being happy but it has not.

Therapist: Test the word marriage...

I'm stuck with this marriage.... that makes sense so the word marriage **is** a nominalisation...

I'm stuck with this married...does not make sense so that is the denominalised form...

Therapist's possible response...

Therapist: So what is it about the way you are married that you specifically do not like?

Jethro: You can also denominalise when working asynchronously too. I have sometimes seen emails that have so many nominalised words in them that I am tempted to use the term **nominalised person**;

the writer has created a world that is totally stuck, by using many nominalisations. Here's an example…

I used to be the one in the family that provided guidance to the others and look into the problems that they brought to me. But because of my enthusiasm for my new job it was as if I had taken my job responsibilities and transferred them to my family. This meant that I started to compromise the reputation and position of my family in the community because of the decisions I was making. I even noticed that I was using the same assessment process that I used at work to carry out assessments on my own friends and I would hear their circumstances as if I was their boss. I hate what has happened to me….

Jethro: Did you spot the nominalisations there…?
.
Here they are. You may even find some that I haven't underlined…

I used to be the one in the family that provided <u>guidance</u> to the others and look into the <u>problems</u> that they brought to me. But because of my <u>enthusiasm</u> for my new job it was as if I had taken my job <u>responsibilities</u> and transferred them to my family. This meant that I started to <u>compromise</u> the <u>reputation</u> and <u>position</u> of my family in the <u>community</u> because of the <u>decisions</u> I was making. I even noticed that I was using the same <u>assessment process</u> that I used at work to carry out <u>assessments</u> on my own friends and I would hear their <u>circumstances</u> as if I was their boss. I hate what has happened to me….

Jethro: And a denominalised response…

Jane, I can hear from your last email that you are so enthusiastic about your new job that you have been transferring some aspects of what you feel responsible for, onto your family. You mentioned too, that you have started assessing your friends and family in certain ways. I wonder which friends you have been assessing and how have you been doing it? I hear that you feel that you have positioned yourself differently with your friends and family and I wonder what you could start to do differently yourself, so that you have repositioned yourself in a way that you feel that you are no longer compromising...

Jethro: In actual fact it's quite rare to get someone who uses so many nominalisations in such a short paragraph so my denominalised response may seem a little unreal, but I hope it shows you how you can denominalise in an email. There are, however, some people are highly nominalised in their language patterns and this could be an indication that they have set up for themselves a nominalised world. By denominalising, you can get them back to a model of the world that is unstuck...

So before we move on, let's have a quiz to see if you can recognise nominalisations and then respond to them...

Which of the following words are nominalisations?

Trust
Responsibility
Forgiveness
Process
Peaceful
Enthusiasm
Powerful
Humour
Beauty
Understand
Efficiency
Delightful
Balance
Education

Nominalisations in bold ☺

Trust
Responsibility
Forgiveness
Process
Peaceful
Enthusiasm
Powerful
Humour
Beauty
Understand
Efficiency
Delightful
Balance
Education

Jethro: And another. How would you respond to these?

He has a lot of anger

Mark: Who is he angry with?

You don't respect me

Ali: How am I not respecting you?

We need to improve our communication

Hag: How do we need to improve the way we are communicating?

I have no courage

Baz: So how specifically are not courageous?

Jethro: In addition, once you have recognised the nominalisation and have denominalised it, you can respond by asking who is nominalising about what, and how they are doing it...

By responding to your client in a denominalised format, you will be sending messages to them that the world they are creating, the nominalised world, can be more fluid and changeable than they perceive. This is a great way of allowing the stuck client to change the meaning of their stuckness, with your help, to a world that has some possibility for change and I guess that's part of what we all do here.

Hag: It took me a while but I got there in the end.

Jethro: That's good. Let's take a well-earned break and continue later.

Chapter 6.

Asking more questions online

Jethro: Welcome back again.... We have explored examples of generalisation and deletions. One final example we can explore is when words or sentences contain **distortions...**

I would like you to have a look at this section of text and let me know what you can glean from it...

Well I can't help knowing that my wife is at the end of her tether with me. She thinks I am so thoughtless. Let me tell you what happened the other day. I went to the supermarket in the car to get some items that my wife told me she wanted for her party. As I drove into the car park at the supermarket, I swerved my car to avoid a driver in a red BMW. I could see the face of the woman driver and I knew that she had other things on her mind other than driving. I had to put my brakes on with such a force that the brakes screeched. I saw a man nearby pushing a shopping trolley. He looked so angry that I knew he must have wanted to have a go at me. As for the woman in the red BMW, she was so pretentious in her red car and red suit. I know what makes a person like that tick. It's money, money and more money. She mouthed something at me as I drove past her and I knew that my calm expression only made her angrier. When I got home I realised that I had completely forgotten to buy the things for my wife's party. When my wife had asked me if I had done the shopping I said that I hadn't been yet and that I had just been out to test the brakes on the car. She looked at me knowing I was covering up my near accident with the red BMW. If my wife really cared for me she would know that I do the best I can for her.

Hag: The guy is scared of his wife! LOL.

Jethro: That's one thing you might suppose and I could certainly share that one with you, but as we are considering a linguistic approach to therapy, have a look at the text and then consider what he has written.

Man: He seems to be assuming a lot of things about what other people are thinking.

Jethro: Exactly, look at the following underlined extracts from the bulk of the text…

<u>Well I can't help knowing that my wife is at the end of her tether with me.</u> <u>She thinks I am so thoughtless.</u> Let me tell you what happened the other day. I went to the supermarket in the car to get some items that my wife told me she wanted for her party. As I drove into the car park at the supermarket I swerved my car to avoid a driver in a red BMW. <u>I could see the face of the woman driver and I knew that she had other things on her mind other than driving.</u> I had to put my brakes on with such a force that the brakes screeched. I saw a man nearby pushing a shopping trolley. <u>He looked so angry that I knew he must have wanted to have a go at me.</u> As for the woman in the red BMW, she was so pretentious in her red car and red suit. <u>I know what makes a person like that tick.</u> It's money, money and more money. She mouthed something at me as I drove past her and <u>I knew that my calm expression only made her angrier</u>. When I got home I realised that I had completely forgotten to buy the things for my wife's party. When my wife had asked me if I had done the shopping I said that I hadn't been yet and that I had just been out to test the brakes on the car. <u>She looked at me knowing I was covering up my near accident with the red BMW.</u> <u>If my wife really cared for me she would know that I do the best I can for her.</u>

Jethro: I have underlined examples of **Mind Reading**, or believing that you know someone's internal state. Mind reading is an example of when someone makes a distortion about the other person's state. They assume that the person is thinking thoughts or feeling certain feelings…

The way to work with mind reading when your client shows it in their emails or in the chat exchange is to ask the simple question…

How do you know?

Man: When my partner is angry I can tell. Does that mean I am mind reading?

Jethro: Well you may be able to assume that his behaviour is similar to previous times when you know he was previously angry, and therefore be able to label his latest behaviour as angry behaviour, but you will never be able to really know what he is feeling or what he is in fact thinking, you wont be able to hear his internal dialogue or have any idea if he is making any images in his head or what those images might be.

Geraldine: In the last example in the BMW story that "mind read" seems to be different to the others.

Jethro: Yes, that's true, in a way it's a reverse mind read as it presupposes that his wife should be able to read his mind. **I know this as reverse mind reading**. The response is still the same as with straightforward mind reading by asking ...

How do you know?

Mark: I think that I have a client that does a lot of mind reading.

Ali: How do you know? LOL.

Jethro: Well if you feel you are ok with recognising mind reading in the bulk of text and feel you know how to respond to it, let's go further shall we...?

Earlier on in the workshop we talked about how matching a belief can help build rapport. Of course it's possible that a client may have a limiting belief about themselves, about others or the world. If this is the case then it may be useful for the therapist to challenge the client's limiting belief. As we have discussed previously, beliefs are generally expressed in text as either a "this means that", a complex equivalence, or a "this causes that", a cause effect...

Let's have a further look at these two examples of how beliefs are expressed shall we...?

In a **complex equivalence,** two statements can be expressed in a way that seems to indicate that both elements of the statement mean the same...

For example...

You don't love me because you are not listening to me.

Jethro: The assumption here is the belief that listening is the same as loving...

Often a complex equivalence will have a pattern of

Behaviour is equal to emotion...

In this case, the behaviour is listening and the emotion is loving...

The simplest way to challenge a belief in the form of a complex equivalence in this way is to feedback the question...

"How does this mean that?"

Or...

"How does listening mean loving?"...

I wonder how many of you here have the belief that listening is the same as loving.

Mark: Well it would mean that a deaf person could never fall in love.

Jethro: That's a wonderful way of responding, and that is a more subtle way of changing someone's belief rather than responding by saying " How does listening mean loving" This is a really good example of how we can **reframe** the statements that are made by clients in text to enable them to look again at their beliefs. However, for now, let's just stick with the simple response of how does a mean b?

We can build on this later.

What about the other way that beliefs are expressed in text?

What about the cause effect...?

My husband makes me sad

You bore me to death

You make me sick

Those bacteria will kill me

Jethro: I have listed some cause effects here and you may already see that some of these beliefs may be limiting to the person expressing them...

The way to respond to such cause effects is to use the question

How does this cause that?

Let's have a look at one shall we?

My husband makes me sad

This statement implies that there is something that the husband does that makes the person sad. It alludes to the fact that the person making the statement has no choice in the matter and in a way it says...

My husband forces me to be sad...

Of course the question "How specifically does your husband force you to be sad?" can allow you as a therapist, to indicate to the client, that he or she probably has some responsibility how they feel. It can open up a discussion that as the husband is not actually forcing the client to be sad and that the client can have some choice in the matter. Giving a client more choice is a good option in a therapeutic alliance. It can point out to the client that they have some responsibility and control over how they feel...

So if you were working synchronously, you could respond with the direct question of "How does this cause that?", but if you are working using email exchange, you may want to embed the question in a reply like this...

I hear that your husband makes you feel sad and I wondered just exactly what your husband does to **make** you feel sad. When you say that he makes you feel sad it conjures up an image for me where he's actually forcing you to be sad, and I wondered if you ever thought that you may have a different way of responding to what he does, so that instead of him making you feel sad, you may choose to have a different response instead?

Baz: So the client may respond by saying that when he hits me it makes me feel sad.

Jethro: Hitting someone is not generally acceptable behaviour unless you are in the boxing fraternity, so if that was the response to the question "How does your husband cause you to be sad?", you can still respond in the same way by letting the client know that the husband hasn't forced her to be sad and that she can have other options. - She could be angry, or determined or assertive or courageous and if those choices were there too they may give forth a different behavioural response by the client...

So let's move on...

When we were looking at deletions earlier, we explored comparative deletions. This is when a comparison is being made but there is no indication of what the comparison is being made against.

One example of this is...

Spiderman is stronger...

The statement does not state who Spiderman is stronger than and so we call it a comparative deletion.

Ali: They feel like judgement statements to me.

Jethro: In effect, they are and that's why I have revisited them, as I want you to consider this...

It's wrong to say that.

Man: Who says it's wrong to say that?

Jethro: Yes, well done, now in my experience I do not think I have come across this pattern often in online work. I'm not sure why and perhaps someone here would like to spend some time researching that one. However I would like you to notice it here and get accustomed to it, just in case your clients change the way they communicate with you and suddenly send you texts and emails with these judgements in them. These statements do not seem to be often used when writing emails or letters, but are often used in conversation. As synchronous work is closer to a conversation than email exchange I think that if they do come up, they are more likely to come up in that format than in email exchange...

Let's meet up again tomorrow shall we as I feel that you have understood that last example really well.

Chapter 7.

The unwritten lines.

Jethro: Welcome back, I hope you all had a great evening and were able to gain maximum experience from your process of relaxation and enjoyment....

This morning we are going to look at how certain text structures can allow you to see what is not written directly in text communication, and then, to use what is not written to help your client make changes.

Ali: It sounds like magic.

Jethro: Well, in a way it is a little like that because we will learn how to see what is invisible, and that's got to be a little bit magical I guess...

Let's start by looking at a line of text. This could be either in the body of an email or be sent to you in a chat window...

If he hits me again, I will have to leave him.

Jethro: So, in order for that sentence to be true **for the client**, what must be true in that line of text?

Man: That her husband hits her.

Jethro: Well can you see anything in the text that presupposes that the person hitting is a husband?

Man: Erm..well no, that's a good point. I just generated that illusion in my head.

Jethro: That's good, because I know that sometimes when people read text, they can generate links that are not there, so it's worthwhile looking at this line again and asking this question...

In order for that sentence to be true for the client, what must be true for the client in that line of text?

Man: Well I'm so used to the concept of a man hitting a woman that I failed to realise that this could be a man hitting a woman, or a man hitting a man. So the only thing I can see in that line of text that fits your criteria is that a man has hit the listener.

Jethro: Yes, that's good; do any of you notice anything else?

Man: That the person doing the hitting has done it before.

Jethro: How do you know?

Man: Because the person uses the term "again" so this presupposes that if the sentence is true for the writer, then the hitting must have happened before.

Jethro: Yes that's good. You got that one. So that's the invisible snippet in that little line. The writer did not say that the person had hit the other person before but it is presupposed in the text, without it being written.

Let's have a look at another one...

My teacher is pregnant and I'm worried that it will cause problems for me later on in the year.

Jethro: So what can you presuppose from that line that must be true for the client. Remember that it's about looking at the text and deducing what must be true for the client and not necessarily for you or for anyone else.

Ali: That the teacher is a woman.

Man: That there is a connection between the teacher being pregnant and problems for the writer in the future.

Hag: That the writer is a student.

Jethro: Yes, so can you see that there are certain aspects of the writer's model of the world that are not overtly stated but can be deduced from the invisible sections in the text...?

Have a go at this one...

The green wombats are stealing my pancakes but the yellow ones just sit there and sing songs.

Man: Well I'd certainly have my concerns about this client! LOLOL.

Jethro: Yes, I thought you may react that way, but if you look at the text, then what must be true for the writer here?

Baz: Well there are wombats of more than one colour.

Mark: The man has more than one pancake.

Ali: The yellow wombats are capable of assuming a sitting position.

Geraldine: The yellow wombats can sing.

Hag: And they can sing more than one song.

Jethro: So, can you see that you are now collecting a lot more information about what must be true for the client for this sentence to be true? A sentence has to have at least a noun and a verb and the rest of the structure can contain adjectives, more nouns etc...

When you can look into the lines of text, and deduce what is presupposed by the client, you can use the presuppositions to gather more information about the client's model of the world, and remember too, that it's probably not the same as your model of the world, unless you all have pancake stealing wombats hanging around...

Once you have learned to presuppose what must be true for the client, you can feedback lines to the client to challenge the client's worldview....

There are options here on how you can choose to respond to what is presupposed in the client's text, the first way to respond is to...

Determine what is presupposed...

Feedback that what is presupposed to the client...

Client: If my husband knew how much I love him, he wouldn't be so mean to me.

Jethro: What does the client presuppose to be true?

Baz: That the husband does not know how much she loves him...

That he is mean to her...

That there is a relationship between how mean he is and how much she loves him.

Jethro: Good. The therapist could then reply...

Client: If my husband knew how much I love him, he wouldn't be so mean to me.

Therapist: How do you know that he does not know how much he loves you?

Or

Therapist: How specifically is your husband mean to you?

Or

Therapist: So are you saying that if he knew you loved him more, he would certainly be less mean to you?

Hag: Now that I have been looking at this exercise, I have suddenly realised how all the other stuff we have explored can come together. I am looking at the text and asking myself certain questions that relate to our earlier work.

Baz: Me too.

Jethro: OK, that's a good sign; can you give me examples of other questions you may want to ask this client?

Man: I detected that the person was mind reading in the statement, as she said "If my husband knew how much I loved him", so I may respond by asking "How do you know that he does not know" because I saw it as a mind read rather than what was presupposed.

Jethro: Yes. So you got to the question via another route and if you have that flexibility then that's a plus.

Ali: I focused on the word "mean" and wanted to ask "How specifically is he mean to you?", in order to uncover the deletion there.

Hag: And the fact that he is mean to her seems to be because he doesn't know she loves him so that implies a cause effect relationship.

Jethro: We can utilise presuppositions to help support the client make changes. Have a look at these examples...

Jane, I wonder what you will do differently as a result of our work today?

Geraldine: Well that presupposes that the client Jane will do something different.

Jethro: And this one...

Jane, I wonder how long it will take you before you can incorporate this new learning into your life.

Mark: That Jane will incorporate new learning into her life.

Jethro: Yes, that's good, and so presuppositions can be very powerful when used this way as they can send a signal in the text that the therapist has presupposed certain things about the therapeutic connection that will allow the client to change in a positive way...

So as you build on what we have learned today about what is presupposed, and add the previous skills we have explored, you can build on your learning so you can have choices in the way you approach the text and increase the variety of your responses.

Man: I have also noticed that when you talk briefly at the start or end of the workshops, you tend to have more nominalisations in your words.

Hag: Learning...choices....approach...variety...responses. Yes I'm getting some of that too LOL.

Jethro: So now that you have increased your understanding with this stuff, perhaps we could have a little quiz. Let me provide you with a series of statements and we can discuss them and look at how you would respond. As before, they will generally be one-liners but they all could form the part of a bulk message in an email too...

Let's practice...

He thinks we are not interested in making changes

Man: How does he know we are not interested?

It's wrong to be like that.

Hag: Who says?

Geraldine: Like what?

My husband makes me so angry.

Mark: What is it that your husband does that forces you to be angry?

I know you don't love me because you don't listen to me.

Hag: How does listening mean the same as loving?

Orchids are expensive.

Ali: Compared to what?

Baz: All orchids?

You are getting worse.

Geraldine: Worse than whom?

I have to do it alone.

Man: What makes you?

Mark: What would happen if you didn't?

I can't finish it on time.

Man: What stops you?

Mark: What would happen if you did?

My decision was terrible.

Hag: What were you deciding?

She is so mean to me.

Ali: How specifically is she so mean to you

I am stressed.

Mark: In what way are you stressed?

They don't give a damn.

Geraldine: Who doesn't?

If my parrot talks to me again like that, I will have to move back to Bolivia.

Hag: The writer has a parrot and it can talk.

The parrot can talk in a way identified by the writer.

Mark: The parrot has talked to the writer in a certain way before...

The act of the parrot talking again will force the writer to move...

The writer has been to Bolivia before.

Baz: So, in what way does the parrot talk to you?

Geraldine: So you are saying that if the parrot talks to you in that way again, you will be **forced** to move back to Bolivia?

Jethro; I can see that you have a good understanding of this process and I know that once you have used these skills, you will be able to become even better therapists and generate much more rewarding interactions with your clients.

Geraldine: And that presupposes that we are already good therapists!

Jethro: Exactly ☺

Chapter 8.

Recognising and changing beliefs online.

Jethro: We have previously spent some time looking at how matching beliefs can be a way of building rapport....

We have already examined the fact that beliefs are not usually expressed in the format "I believe", because that would be too easy....

Instead, we humans tend to express our beliefs in the formats of "this means that" and "this causes that". We have previously looked at how recognising such language patterns can be the key to finding a belief and then, as a way of building rapport, matching those beliefs....

However, sometimes you will get a client presenting beliefs that are causing them pain, are not helpful to them and are linked to why they made their initial contact with you...

So now we are going to look at how to change beliefs that are expressed online....

Let me start by taking two examples of a belief that may be presented to you, either as a one line exchange, for instance in a chat window, or as part of a longer paragraph in an email.

1) When he walks into the room I feel sick.

2) Because you don't listen to what I say, you don't love me.

Jethro: The above lines could be part of a communication to you. Do you have any comments at this stage?

Man: Well I can see that number one is a "this causes that", when he walks into the room it *makes* me feel sick.

Hag: And the other one, number two, is a "this means that" as the writer is saying, "When you don't listen to me it *means* you don't love me.

Jethro: Great, you noticed that my two examples were from the two different forms of expressing beliefs in text, which we have discussed before, namely "this means that" and "this causes that"...

Let's work through all the possible ways you can respond when working towards changing a belief, if they are presented this way. Personally I find that what we are going to explore, works well with email, but it works even better when using a chat format because often a rapid response by the therapist can really get the client to think about their beliefs...

But before we do that, I would like you to have a closer look at the two forms of how beliefs are structured in text.

Let's go back to "this causes that" and the example above

When he walks into the room I feel sick.

I would like you to consider this statement of belief as being made up of two parts.

Mark: The cause and the effect.

Jethro: That's right, and as you look at it, you may notice that in this example, the first part is behaviour, the person walking in the room is making behaviour, and the second section, the effect, is a feeling or an internal response. So this sentence indicates that we have a behaviour causing an internal response for the writer...

Now let's have a look at the other one, the "this means that" and let's do the same with that slice of belief.

Because you don't listen to what I say, you don't love me.

Geraldine: The sentence shows that the first section means the same as the second section.

Jethro: Yes, and if we look at the sentence, you may notice that the first section is behaviour, in this case it is a little subtle but the act of listening is behaviour don't you agree?

Man: And the second section is an emotion.

Jethro: Yes, the sentence is constructed in the format of a behaviour means an internal response....

So when you become even more skilled at noticing that you have a limiting belief from a client, and that belief is structured in the form of a "this causes that" or a "this means that", you may also be able to notice that one side of the sentence may be a behaviour and the other side may have an internal response. We can use our awareness of this to respond to the client in a way that their belief may be changed or at least questioned and be made more fluid or malleable, so that further questions may change the belief...

So now you have even more insight into the formation and structure of beliefs in text, I would like you to consider these examples and how you could respond...

The first option is that you can **change the meaning of the behaviour that is presented...**

Let's look at **reframing the external behaviour...**

I have highlighted the external behaviour in the two examples below...

When he **walks into the room** I instantly feel sick.

I wonder if it's really about him walking into the room that makes you feel sick or is it your thoughts about what you think will happen.

Because he doesn't **listen** to what I say, he doesn't love me.

Could it be that he loves you but he just wants a little time to be quiet whilst you vent your feelings?

Jethro: The second option is closely linked to the first in the way we can **reframe the second part of the belief, the internal response**...

Again I have highlighted the internal response that can be reframed...

When he walks into the room I instantly **feel sick**

Perhaps you don't physically feel sick but you feel sickened by what happened before?

Because he doesn't listen to what I say, he doesn't **love** me

I wonder if he loves you so much that he feels he needs to focus on his own thoughts of you for a while.

Jethro: Another way of responding is to **feedback the external behaviour or the internal response to the person who made the statement, and use their words to change or weaken their belief.**

Let's look at the external behaviour in these two examples...

When he **walks into the room** I instantly feel sick

It sounds like having this belief is allowing him to walk all over you

Because he **doesn't listen** to what I say, he doesn't love me

Well I wonder if you are turning a deaf ear to how he may be feeling.

Ali: I felt angry when I read the first response.

Jethro: That's an interesting response, can you tell me more?

Ali: Well the feedback section "walking all over you" seemed worse than "walking into the room".

Jethro: Well I can see that, and yet perhaps if this person received that response, they may also get angry and use that new feeling to make changes. This client may have felt afraid before, but now may have a new belief that may be expressed as, "he's not going to walk over me anymore"...

Now let's apply the same rule to the **client's internal response...**

When he walks into the room I **instantly feel sick**

Could that be a sick thing to say about him?

Because he doesn't listen to what I say, he **doesn't love me**

I wonder if he would see your comments as unloving.

Jethro: Now let's, for a second or two assume that if someone has a certain belief, even if it is limiting them in some way, that **it must be doing something for them that is positive,** or in some way giving them a secondary gain for holding onto that belief.

Man: But if I had a belief that taking heroin makes me happy, how would that be a positive thing for me?

Jethro: Well you are possibly saying that because you know how hard it can be for you to quit.

Man: I can see that response could make me think differently about what I said, but I don't think it would stop me being a heroin addict.

Jethro: Well it's good to know that my response, which was done using the example we are going to look at, actually got you to think differently about your belief. To get someone to stop being addicted to heroin could take many interactions, challenges, family and support agency interventions but even so, if you did have someone with an addiction problem and you used that pattern, you may start to get them to look at themselves differently. Perhaps by starting to change their belief from "I take heroin because it makes me happy" to "I say it makes me happy because I know that's easier than saying how difficult it has been in the past to quit"...

So let's look at **the positive intent** that could be behind the two statements we are working on.

When he walks into the room I instantly feel sick.

Could it be that your feelings allow you to avoid resolving this issue you have had for a while now?

Because he doesn't listen to what I say, he doesn't love me.

Could it be that you feel unloved and so you are saying this about him?

Jethro: So if someone has a limiting belief, eventually there will **be negative consequences that come from having that belief...**

Often a person may use limiting beliefs in their email or text exchanges because that's how they feel about the situation in the here and now. Feeding back the long-term consequences of their beliefs can also have an impact on how they see the belief. Oh, and it's sometimes a good introduction to start by stating "If you continue to think this way", because that opener really does lead the person to think about how having this belief for a long period of time will affect them...

When he walks into the room I instantly feel sick.

And so if you continue to think this way, you will never be able to talk to him.

Because he doesn't listen to what I say, he doesn't love me.

And if you continue to think this way, when he's engrossed in something you will believe that he doesn't love you again.

Jethro: And of course, having such a belief can lead to the client **having another outcome that they may not have considered...**

By feeding back to the client that their belief is not the real issue here, but there is another one they have not realised, it may allow them to rethink their old belief. You can start this by talking about what is the "real issue" for them...

When he walks into the room I instantly feel sick.

Could it be that the real issue here is about how you use this feeling to avoid conflict?

Because he doesn't listen to what I say, he doesn't love me.

Could it be that the real issue here is about how the two of you communicate with each other?

Jethro: Have you ever noticed that some people have the ability to focus on the really small aspects of a task? They have that ability to make sure that the little things are not overlooked, and they are really good at dotting the "I's" and crossing the "T's". On the other hand, have you ever noticed that some people are really often infuriated by all that minute stuff and for them; they prefer to inhabit a world where they have big ideas and concepts? These people can often be creative, but they are not always good at putting their ideas into action, as they get bored with the small stuff. Yet the ones that are good with the small stuff can make that happen, it's just that often they do not come up with the idea originally.

Geraldine: Well it sounds like you may be describing me.

Jethro: Which one?

Geraldine: I'm really not that much of an ideas person but if someone gives me a task, then I can make sure it's totally completed down to the letter. Also I'm a great proof reader!!

Jethro: Anyone identify with the other option?

Baz: Yes I have been told that I am good in a team because I can come up with some really creative ideas, but when I am allocated tasks that relate to my idea, I struggle with the small stuff and often get pulled up by others for making silly mistakes or going off the boil with a project when its almost completed.

Jethro: So you are probably a big chunk person. Now these two aspects of a someone's preferred style are not in themselves bad or good, but often a person can have a belief that may be nested in the concept of it being either too big or too small, and it may be that your client will do this because of their preference for working in big chunks or small chunks...

We can use this concept of changing the chunk size to get someone to look at their belief statements and hopefully, use the chunks to make changes in their beliefs. We can either **chunk up** to a bigger picture or we can **chunk down** to more detail.

Let's start by **chunking down**...

One way of chunking down or getting down to the specifics is to ask directly "how specifically" as this is a great way of getting down to specifics!

When he walks into the room I instantly feel sick.

How specifically does that happen?

Hag: So if he put just one toe in the room would that make you feel sick too?

Jethro: Yes, that's a more subtle use of chunking down and a good example. Tell me how you did that.

Hag: Well I thought of how the person's behaviour could be made smaller and in this case I thought of the person walking into the room and then just saw the toe entering the room. I then realised that this was a smaller chunk than the whole of the person entering the room, so I used that example.

Jethro: Good, and would you say that you were a big chunk or a small chunk person.

Hag: Well I'm so small chunk it's unbelievable. My family often tell me how I never miss a trick when it comes to the tiny aspects of a problem.

Jethro: Let's have look at this example...

Because he doesn't listen to what I say, he doesn't love me.

Jethro: Would you like to have a go at this one too?

Hag: Well I could say, how specifically does this mean that he doesn't love you or I could say, what if he only listened to one word of yours, would that mean he loved you?

Jethro: Yes that's good, you can use the "how specifically" but I can see that you are also using smaller sections of the belief statement to give a small chunk response that could change the belief...

So if we wanted to **chunk up**, to make the bigger picture? We don't want specifics now we want a more global question. The best way to do this is actually to minimise one half of the statement that the client has used and to expand the other side as a big "chunk up" statement, so in effect this can be more powerful as it can include a chunk down and chunk up in the same response...

When he walks into the room I instantly feel sick.

So as soon as his toe enters the room, you will vomit all over the place?

Because he doesn't listen to what I say, he doesn't love me.

So if he doesn't listen to just one word that makes him totally unlovable?

Jethro: One very powerful way of changing a person's belief statement is to do a simple **counter example**.

 Here we can look at the concept of a time when "this didn't mean that", or "this didn't case that" and feed that back to the client...

When he walks into the room I instantly feel sick.

What if you walked into the room, would you expect him to feel sick?

Because he doesn't listen to what I say, he doesn't love me.

Could it be that you stop loving him when you don't listen?

Jethro: When a person states their belief in the format we have been discussing, it is a belief that they have formed from their perception of the world, their model. Of course as we often know only too well, not everyone has the same perception or model of the world. So one way we can get a person to look at their limiting belief is to ask them if they think that **everyone would have that same model** and hence the same behaviour or internal response as them...

Simplistically, you could actually just ask if everyone, or anyone else, would or wouldn't share this belief...

When he walks into the room I instantly feel sick.

And would it be ok if everyone else had that belief?
And can you imagine a world where everyone believed that?

Because he doesn't listen to what I say, he doesn't love me.

And would it be ok if everyone had that belief?

And can you imagine a world where everyone had that belief?

Jethro: Now, as you already know from our earlier sessions, people tend to operate from their cognitive perceptions of the world around them, and so you can challenge those perceptions or gain more information by asking about **how they came to have those perceptions**...

Let's go with the examples again. The responses could apply to both...

When he walks into the room I instantly feel sick.
Because he doesn't listen to what I say, he doesn't love me.

How would you know if that was not true?

When you think about that belief, what do you see, hear, and feel?

Where did you learn that?

Geraldine: I like the question "how do you know if that is not true" I certainly have never used that before when I am working online with a client, and yet I can see that it could have a lot of potential.

Jethro: We have looked at chunking up and chunking down when it comes to examining and reframing beliefs in text, and we can also use another way of changing the frame of reference for the client...

We can do this by **changing the time frame**. In other words we can look at the concept of whether this belief will be the same in a different time, usually in the future...

Often people can feel stuck by their limiting belief, and they see it as an inflexible problem. Perhaps you may wish to think about this, and how nominalisations can also impact on that feeling of stuckness too? What would it be like if someone structured their beliefs with nominalisations?

Mark: Well I would denominalise them and then work with the denominalised form.

Jethro: That's good. I guess that even when the nominalisation has been denominalised, the belief can still appear to a client in a way that it's not only a problem in the here and now, but will be there forever. By changing the time frame, we can get a client to consider that change can take place in due time. One way to consider this option is to think about how the passage of time has changed the world. Consider the advances in medicine and how a few years ago, some illnesses were a "death sentence" but are now widely treatable...

When he walks into the room I instantly feel sick.

And perhaps after learning more about yourself you may feel differently in the future?

Because he doesn't listen to what I say, he doesn't love me.

And perhaps when you have openly discussed this with him you may feel differently when he is silent in the future?

Jethro: Another version of altering the frame of reference for the client is to **add all or nothing statements to your response...**

This is a way of exaggerating the client's belief, and once the client has heard the exaggeration, it may get the client to think differently about what they have said...

When he walks into the room I instantly feel sick.

Can you imagine what a room could end up like if everyone held that belief?

Because he doesn't listen to what I say, he doesn't love me.

I'm sure everyone has had a quiet time when they didn't want to talk. Does that mean they are all unloving?

Jethro: You can also shift the direction of your response to how it would **be if other people had this belief...**

This is similar to the addition of all or nothing responses, but you can focus on specific others in the response, and that could change the client's perspective.

When he walks into the room I instantly feel sick.

And can you imagine it if everyone had that response?

Because he doesn't listen to what I say, he doesn't love me.

And would you like your daughter to have that belief too when she grows up?

Ali: Referring to someone's child like that seems very powerful.

Jethro: It can allow the client to assess whether they are being hypocritical in their belief. If they accept the belief for themselves, and they don't accept it for their children, there is an incongruence there that the therapist can explore further...

I have mentioned before, when we were working on the section on building rapport online, it can be helpful to access a person's values system. In the past we have accessed the client's values system to gain rapport...

Here we can do it to get the client to **challenge his or her own values...**

We reflect back what is important to them. Remember too, that values are those things that are important to us, so here we try and focus on that...

When he walks into the room I instantly feel sick.

What's more important here, the fact he is allowed to walk into a room, or your response to that happening?

Because he doesn't listen to what I say, he doesn't love me.

Isn't it more important to focus on how you can accept how a person is, rather than on the fact that he's focused in on himself occasionally?

Jethro: Later on in our work we shall be looking in depth on how you can use **metaphor and story...**

Now we can just look at how a short metaphor or story response to your client could get them to hold a different belief...

When he walks into the room I instantly feel sick.

Many years ago a scientist taught a dog to salivate when a bell was rung. Even when the dog was older, it still salivated when it heard a bell. It was only after the dog started to get new experiences that were connected to a bell ringing that allowed the dog to gain control back, and not salivate every time a bell rang.

Because he doesn't listen to what I say, he doesn't love me.

My mother once told me a story about a prince that was bullied when he was a child. He would have to hide away from the hurt he felt and then as he grew up he would go into a secret garden whenever he felt hurt. It took the princess many years of patience to find that garden, and even longer for her to be allowed into it with the prince. But once they were there together, the prince knew he had found his soul mate.

Ali: Up to now I was thinking about how useful this work would be when working synchronously as I could see how the responses could be brief, however, I'm not so sure about the last one.

Jethro: Well, yes you are right. Let me add to what you have said. If you consider asynchronous work, you will generally get much more text sent out to you than when you are working synchronously. If you have saved any of your old synchronous text exchanges, you will probably have lots of interactions, made up of sentences that are much shorter than in email exchange, and on many occasions they can also be much shorter than in face-to-face conversations. In face-to-face conversations, a person can speak at length for some considerable time.

Man: Yes I've had that experience LOL.

Jethro: So you will understand perhaps that when people are working synchronously, they generally have more exchanges per hour and have sentences that are shorter than in face-to-face conversation...

Of course the belief change model we have discussed here today is ideal for working synchronously as it can allow you to have a quick response with the client. You can feedback your belief change response as a one-liner. Whether it has an impact on the client or not, will be judged by the client's response. If you work face-to-face with someone and can change his or her beliefs what happens...?

You have gone quiet. Well last week I worked with a client and he said that all beliefs that he learnt as a child would be difficult for him to change...

So I rephrased this by saying...

So you are saying that because you believed something as a child, it will still be with you now you are a man?

Jethro: Before he answered he took a long pause and his eyes moved from side to side, he looked like he was processing the information I had given him

Ali: Could you have gone for saying "all beliefs..."

Jethro: Yes I could have done that, and perhaps that would have been the better initial option. I'm glad you noticed that one...

He replied by saying...

Client: Well there is one particular thing that I learnt as a child that I still believe now, and that is that the world is a dangerous place.

Jethro: How do you know that?

Client: Well only last week a man in my village was murdered.

Jethro: That's not a nice piece of news to get in your village but you are saying that because someone was murdered in your village it means that the world is a dangerous place.

Client: Yes that's it.

Jethro: But when you were a child that person hadn't been murdered then, so how did you come to believe that the world was a dangerous place when you were a child.

Client: Because my brother would often come home from school with a bloody nose and tell me that it was dangerous out there.

Jethro: So it sounds as if your brother had his share of conflicts and you are saying that because your brother often had a bloody nose when he came home it means that the world is a dangerous place.

Client: Yes that's how I learnt it.

Jethro: I wonder if it was you brother that was dangerous rather than the world?

Client: Well I do know he was often called a troublemaker.

Jethro: I have observed that when working face-to-face, a client will take longer to respond if they are processing what you have said to them before they change their belief. It's that "oh yeah, I never thought of that" moment. They can often have changes in skin tone, eye movements etc, whilst processing the change. Of course online it's impossible to notice that, but if you are working synchronously, you may get used to the interaction response from the client and then when you go for a belief change, you may notice that they take longer to respond.

Mark: They could be fiddling with the lamp in their room.

Jethro: Yes that's true so instead of guessing, you could ask...

I noticed you took a little longer than usual to respond to that and I wonder why that was...

Jethro: So these online skills we have explored can be great when working synchronously and even the final one, the use of metaphor can be used synchronously, if you use dots... to let your client know... you are telling a story. You can keep a set of the responses next to you so that when you are working online with your client you can have access to the possible options you could use...

Now in the two examples we have explored, one is a complex equivalence and the other is a cause effect. I would like you to consider the process of how these responses work rather than focusing on the type of belief structure. In fact two days ago someone walked into my room at home and said to me...

If I don't find that sun lotion I will go crazy.

Man: I can't tell if that's a cause effect or a complex equivalence.

Jethro: Good, I'm glad you were honest with that comment as often it can be difficult to tell, but for our work, I am saying that is not that important to know exactly if it's one or the other. If you can get a feel that it is *either* a complex equivalence or a cause effect that's a good start. You should be able to use the responses we have touched on. How could you respond to the above sentence?

Man: It's not just about the sun cream it's more about the fact that you know you have been in this situation before.

Mark: You are not going insane but getting frustrated, and that's natural when someone can't find something.

Ali: This sounds like crazy thinking to me.

Hag: I think your behaviour is a great way of enlisting others to help you find the lotion.

Geraldine: But when you go insane you will no longer worry about where the sun lotion is.

Ali: Why don't you forget that sun lotion and wear that lovely summer hat instead?

Man: And it's important to you that you don't get skin cancer, that's the voice of sanity.

Mark: How does losing one tiny jar of sun lotion lead you to feel that you need to see a psychiatrist?

Jethro: Ok, you seem to be getting the hang of this. I noticed that you were looking at your notes in order to make a response. That's a great way of learning. If you set up a series of cause effects and complex equivalence examples and use the notes to give responses, in as many categories as you can, you will soon learn to use many of the options. And of course the great thing about working online is that you can have notes and aide memoirs next to you when you work with your clients.

Does anyone have a metaphor story for the sun lotion belief?

Ok let me...

A friend of mine was looking for something... he had lost once.... And although his journey started out as fruitless...he discovered an old photo album whilst he was looking...it contained pictures of his family...he became totally engrossed in the album...he became so happy looking at the images in the album that...he forgot all about what he was looking for...because he had found something more important to focus on....

Thank you.

Chapter 9.

Reading cures.

Jethro: Hello again, today we are going to start exploring another aspect of using text when working online. The skills we examine today will be mainly useful to those working asynchronously, using email exchange, because the main body of work generated by the therapist is much larger than in synchronous exchange. However it may be that you could modify the technique for synchronous work by either using dots ….. to let the client know you are still writing or by sending the information in an email to be read after the synchronous session…

May I continue?

Hag: I'm on the edge of my seat ☺

Baz: (using brackets here to indicate an agreeing nod!)

Jethro: Often a client can get a new insight on how they are, and how they want to be, by getting involved in writing about their circumstances. People can spend quite some time, writing and expressing what has happened in their lives, how they are now and possibly, where they want to be in the future….

When a person revisits an experience, and in this case I'm talking about when a client writes about an experience, then the nature of the experience can change for the client. In other words, the very act of writing can facilitate a change because the client gets new insights into what happened. Also they may receive feedback that allows them to feel differently about the experience now…

Writing about the experience, coupled with your interventions, can allow the client to **reframe** how they felt about the experience they had, and how they can use the resources they have now, to make changes. I have heard this process of writing about an experience to facilitate change, being referred to as a "writing cure" and I guess to some extent, that's a very concise way of expressing it...

The act of writing by the client can facilitate change...

Today, however, I want to look at another aspect of working online. This other option is a mirror process to a writing cure. I guess we could refer to this other option as a "reading cure". Today we are going to explore how you can write to the client to facilitate change.

Man: Haven't we been doing that already?

Jethro: Well to a certain extent we have, because even with the one-line responses that we explored yesterday, there has to be an element where the client has to read what we have written, but today we are going to take a little sidestep into how we can write to a client so that when the client reads what we have written, it can facilitate change and new thinking for them...

Do you remember when you were tiny and someone read a story to you. For me personally, I remember well, an occasion at school when every Friday afternoon, the teacher would get the class to sit down in front of her and then she would read a story from a book. Twenty years later, one of the stories was made into a movie and when the concept was being discussed on the radio, I said to myself "I know this story"; I had remembered it, albeit subconsciously for over twenty years. Now I wonder if we could tell stories to our clients.

Ali: I do know that hearing stories can be powerful. I went on a story telling workshop once but it was a little disappointing for me.

Jethro: Go on.

Ali: Well the man who came along was amazing at telling the stories, and I felt that it would be great if I could learn how to do it, but the workshop didn't have a lot of structure to it and so when I came away, I had a great sense of feeling good because I had heard some amazing stories, but I was a little frustrated because I still felt I didn't have the skills to tell stories to others.

Jethro: Ok, that's good to hear because today we are going to explore how to tell stories in a way that could have therapeutic value for the client. This process will allow you to write to a client and hopefully, the story, when read by the client, will have therapeutic value for them. We can look at a model that will allow you to learn how to construct a story. Once you have learnt the model you should, with a little practice be able to construct a story that could be beneficial to the client...

This form of reading cure can be a great way to shift the focus from therapist and client to another object, in this case the story itself. This method can be very effective if you are working with a client that has an issue that is too delicate to discuss directly. I understand that when working online, people can be disinhibited when it comes to what they write, but there are still some people that have issues that will benefit from a less direct approach and this is where story can come in useful...

One very easy way to shift the focus is to use **"my friend John"**, when I say that, I mean to use a technique that refers to someone else as a means of conveying the story. When you do this, you have already shifted the focus...

A friend of mine had an interesting experience....

Someone told me the other day...

I met a man on a training course once....

The above are all examples of how you could start to shift the focus of your narrative to the client in a subtle way.

Hag: It sounds as if we are generating a creative process here for the client.

Jethro: Often people will express their metaphors in synchronous work and the process of metaphor matching applies well to email and chat...

Here's an example...

Client: Its no good, I went off the rails again last week.

Therapist: So you didn't see the light at the end of the tunnel that you expected to see?

Client: No, I think I was the Original Flying Scotsman ☺ [client was from Glasgow].

Therapist: Well I do know you have a tendency to blow off steam when you don't get to your destination ☺

Geraldine: Also it seems like a great way of using humour to build rapport. So the man had a train metaphor going on for him and you connected with it, but would you keep with it?

Jethro: Probably not for the whole journey, but I would note the exchange and I may refer to it again. Not merely as a way of building rapport and humour, but as a possible route to a "reading cure" for the client at a later date...

When I think back to when I was at school, I remember being totally enthralled by stories, and later, when I started reading adventure stories and science fiction, I became totally engrossed in the story to the point where my mum would have to shout at me before I would hear her. So too, when a client can get the opportunity to read a story, they too, will be able to become engrossed in what you have written. If they can have that shift of attention, they may learn about their issues in a different way, and the fact that they can be allowed to become engrossed in a written world that is right for them, can facilitate change. I also think that it's a great way of allowing you to "get in" when a client has been resistant. I like to think that a resistant client occurs when the therapist hasn't gained enough rapport with the client. Storytelling can be a great way to build up that rapport and break down the resistance. It's very difficult to resist something that doesn't apply to them directly. It's hard to do a mental "yes but..." when you are not referring to them, but are referring to frog or a mouse or a train or your friend John.

Man: I have a client that has lots of problems due to the fact that they don't seem to be able to solve problems; it's as if they have not mastered the basics of problem solving. The client has missed the ability to solve problems. I have been having email exchanges with him about this and despite the fact that we have talked about problem solving; it seems to be out of his grasp. I wonder if a story may help him.

Jethro: Well yes I think it could. You could tell a story to the client that's couched as a problem and then as then ask the client to continue the story. How old is the client?

Man: He's in his late 50's.

Jethro: Well I wonder if he's ever seen any of those movies that would have been around when he was a small boy. I'm thinking of the adventure movies such as "The Claw" or "Flash Gordon". Now many people will be too young to relate to those, but if he is in his late 50's he may have seen them as a "b movie". In those films, each episode ended as a cliffhanger, where the hero was trapped, their demise guaranteed, but in the next episode, they managed to rescue themselves from the hot lava or the snake pit. You may wish to tell him a similar tale. Take a "hero" to the point where he/she is in danger and get the client to continue the story. If he can write a continuation where the hero has not died, then he has solved a problem and then you can use that information with him at another session.

Hag: Yes but what if he doesn't allow the hero to be saved?

Jethro: Well I think that would be unlikely, but even if it happened that way, you would end up with useful feedback. You would know the client was able to do and what he was not able to do, what he could change in the story and what he couldn't change. Then you could discuss that, and at a later date, give him another "episode" to see if he could solve another dilemma. You may have to simplify the dilemma so that the problem has a more obvious solution. By that I mean, obvious to you and not so much for the client. Most of the time when I use a story in this way, I do not generate a solution, but instead I leave the solution open for the client to apply.

Geraldine: I have a client that is very intellectual and totally in her head when she is writing to me. I think that writing a story to her would not work at all.

Jethro: Well I understand what you are saying and yet if you can write a story to a client that "lives inside her head", then it can be a great way for the client to start to access her heart and her emotions.

Geraldine: I would be concerned that the story would break down any rapport we have.

Jethro: Well it's understandable for you to be concerned about how a new approach could break down rapport with a client. You may wish to consider using a metaphor that connected more with the client's head first, and then coax her more into a different place as she reads your story. That way you can slowly move her from head to heart as she reads...

Here's an example...

I went to school with a boy who had the most amazing memory. He was so good at remembering facts and figures that he was invited by the school to take part in a national competition to find the most intelligent pupil in England. He loved to read about inventions and how things worked and when he accepted the challenge, he would spend most of his evenings working late and reading. He loved to learn and would spend ages talking to his parents and other adults about the new concepts he had learnt in maths and science.

On the day of the competition, which was in the form of a quiz, he went by train to London where he was ushered into a huge hall where all the other competitors were. As he sat down on a chair, a girl sat next to him. He didn't notice her at first, as he was busy reading about Isaac Newton, but he started to notice the wonderful smell of her dress, a sort of fresh rose tinted perfume smell. He looked up and saw a huge mane of blonde curly hair and the biggest brightest smile. As he looked at her, he felt his heart miss a beat and he felt as if his knees had gone all wobbly. She said "hello" and as he replied, his words wouldn't come out properly. He just stuttered and mumbled. He felt as if his world had been turned upside down. He managed a few grunts and then she smiled again and said her name was Zoë. He just nodded, speechless, as he looked into her big blue eyes. A teacher came along and told him that he had to move to another section of the room. He walked with the teacher and sat down at another set of chairs and tables, but instead of reading about Isaac Newton, he was still looking if he could see Zoë in the crowd...

Man: So you have started a story that focuses on intellect and brains and then moved into a tale about the boys first ever crush?

Jethro: Well essentially, yes, and this story could have been extended so that the reader became even more able to make that shift from intellect to feelings...

Let's talk about VAKOG now.

Hag: Is that an item of Scandinavian furniture? LOL.

Jethro: I think we have touched on this before and yes, it could also be a Scandinavian insult too, and I don't want to insult anyone from Scandinavia...

When I say VAKOG, I'm referring to...

Visual – what you see
Auditory – what you hear
Kinaesthetic – what you feel
Olfactory- what you smell
Gustatory-what you taste

I mention these here because they are all important when writing a story. Using VAKOG will allow you to make your stories more alive when you write to a client.

Mark: I'm just thinking that if I write a story to one of my clients it will take me ages, well over the scheduled one-hour appointment.

Jethro: Well perhaps that may happen at first, but as you get into them you will find that you can construct a story relatively quickly, and of course you can save your stories so that you can **cut and paste** them if they apply to other people. Of course they may need some modification, but it will still save you time. It's worth having a stock of stories that you can tweak, so they are more tailored to the individual...

Let's have a look at what it's like to add VAKOG...

Before VAKOG...

He walked into the shop and sat down in a chair that was nearby. After a while a man came into the shop from the street. He had come in from the side door, and he also sat down in the room.

Jethro: After added VAKOG...

He walked into the shop, noticing the fusty smell of old magazines and sat down in a nearby red leather chair with studded brass upholstery pins lined up along its edges. He sank deeply into such an amazingly comfortable chair. After a while, a man with a goatee beard and rimless spectacles came into the shop from the busy street. As he opened and closed the door, he allowed a snippet of traffic noise to enter the previously quiet surroundings...

Jethro: So you can see that in the second example, I have added some VAKOG, well to be honest I didn't add any G – taste, but I could have made a reference to some food if that was important. Usually the VAK are the most common ingredients to add in order to make your story more engaging and alive. So you may wish to consider the model of adding VAKOG, if you are going to write this way.

Mark: Yes, I agree that the second tale with added VAKOG was so much more engaging.
Ali: Now I realise that the storyteller I saw once, added a lot of VAKOG and I wasn't aware of it. I just felt captivated by the story.

Jethro: Yes and the VAKOG is part of the toolkit that allows you to do that...

So let's assume that you would like to consider writing to a client so that the client may access what you write, and hence what they read, in a therapeutic way. In the example above, where the client and the therapist were involved with a train metaphor, you may have observed how well those short one-line responses would have suited synchronous counselling. However, the process I am now going to explain would almost certainly be exclusive to email exchange...

Let's assume that you are going to create a metaphor story for a client to read...

First of all you need to be at a point in your work with the client where you can be aware of the client's history, and the presenting problems. For that reason, I wouldn't recommend that you send a metaphor story to a client in your first or second email...

Here's a very brief case history and the presenting problem for a client...

The client is a 32-year-old woman. She met her partner when she was 16 and fell in love with him. He is now 52 and she was attracted to him because he was able to allow her to move out of her home. She hated living at home as her mum and dad were both alcoholics, and so she had to virtually care for them when they were too drunk to look after themselves. He was 36 at the time and had his own house and car. He works in computing and she was doing computer studies at school when they met. At first they would often spend quality time working on computers, and she still has a passion for computing and the Internet. However, he became so busy at work that he stopped spending any time with her...

After being married for a few months, her husband became very possessive and jealous. He kept suspecting that she was interested in other men. He wouldn't let her go to college to study and would get very angry if she went out of the house during the day when he was at work...

After a while he became violent to her, and later on he started drinking...

Now she's 32 and he's 52. She feels that any love she had for him has long gone...

He insists that she stays home and cooks, cleans and irons his clothes for him. He will often come home late and drunk. He demands that his dinner is ready as soon as he gets home, even though she has no idea when he's coming home. He has hit her several times and each time he is violent to her, he seems to be more aggressive. She has had black eyes and bruised ribs on several occasions...

She now wants to leave him and has noticed, from her online searches, that there are safe houses where women that are being physically abused, can go for support and protection. However, she feels too ashamed to make any enquiries and she also feels that at 32, she is too old to leave him and learn new skills, to get a job and support herself...

Here's the first stage...

Ok, so we have an overview of the client's history. Now the first stage is to **select the nouns** in the case history. I wouldn't worry too much if you miss a few, but as long as you can detect most of them, you will probably have enough to create the metaphor. Here's my attempt. I've highlighted them in **bold**

The client is a 32-year-old **woman**. She met her **partner** when she was 16 and fell in love with him. He is now 52 and she was attracted to him because he was able to allow her to move out of her **home**. She hated living at **home** as her **mum and dad** were both **alcoholics** and so she had to virtually care for them when they were too drunk to look after themselves. He was 36 at the time and had his own **house and car**. He works in computing and she was doing **computer** studies at school when they met. At first they would often spend quality time working on **computers** and she still has a passion for computing and the Internet. However, he became so busy at work that he stopped spending any time with her.

After being married for a few months, her partner became very possessive and jealous. He kept suspecting that she was interested in other **men.** He wouldn't let her go to **college** to study and would get very angry if she went out of the **house** during the day when he was at work.

After a while he became violent to her and later on he started drinking.

Now she's 32 and he's 52. She feels that any love she had for him has long gone.

He insists that she stays **home** and cooks, cleans and irons his **clothes** for him. He will often come **home** late and drunk. He demands that his **dinner** is ready as soon as he gets **home**, even though she has no idea when he's coming **home**. He has hit her several times and each time he is violent to her, he seems to be more aggressive. She has had black **eyes** and bruised **ribs** on several occasions.

She now wants to leave him and has noticed, from her online searches, that there are **safe houses** where **women** that are being physically abused can go for support and protection. However, she feels too ashamed to make any enquiries and she also feels that at 32, she is too old to leave him and learn new skills to get a **job** and support her.

And now the second stage...

So that's my attempt at highlighting the nouns in this case study. Next I need to highlight the process words, **the verbs**. I have highlighted by **underlining the words**, you will also need to include any **nominalisations** too, as they are verbs that have been distorted into nouns...

The client is a 32-year-old **woman**. She **met** her **partner** when she was 16 and **fell in love** with him. He is now 52 and she **was attracted** to him because he was able **to allow her to move out** of her **home**. She **hated living** at home as her **mum and dad** were both **alcoholics** and so she had to virtually **care** for them when they were too **drunk to look after** themselves. He was 36 at the time and **had** his own **house and car**. He **works** in computing and she was **doing computer studies** at school when they **met.** At first they would often **spend** quality time **working** on **computers** and she still has a passion for **computing** and the Internet. However, he became so busy at work that he **stopped** spending any time with her.

After being **married** for a few months, her partner became very **possessive and jealous**. He kept **suspecting** that she was **interested** in other **men**. He wouldn't **let her go** to **college to study** and would **get very angry** if she **went** out of the **house** during the day when he **was** at **work**.

After a while he **became violent** to her and later on he started **drinking.**

Now she's 32 and he's 52. She feels that any **love** she had for him has long gone.

He insists that she **stays home** and **cooks, cleans and irons** his **clothes** for him. He will often **come** home late and **drunk.** He **demands** that his **dinner** is ready as soon as he gets **home,** even though she has no idea when he's coming **home**. He has **hit** her several times and each time **he is violent** to her, **he seems to be**

more aggressive. She has had black **eyes** and bruised **ribs** on several occasions.

She now wants **to leave** him and has **noticed,** from her online **searches**, that there are **safe houses** where **women** that **are being physically abused** can **go** for **support and protection**. However, she **feels** too ashamed to **make any enquiries** and she also **feels** that at 32, she is too old **to leave** him **and learn** new skills to get a **job** and **support** her...

Now I'm not sure if I have got all these nouns and verbs exactly correct, but as long as you can be near enough, you do not need to be perfect with this process...

And now to the third stage...

So now we have to find a **mapped over world** for the story to be set in. I know that this client is interested in computing so that's an option, but I think that computing will not be distant enough for the client. Has anyone got any ideas where we could place a story for this client?

Mark: Well the story almost had a Cinderella aspect to it when I heard that she had to stay in a work whilst he was out drinking.

Jethro: Yes, I can see how you would consider that. And yet I would not choose to mention Cinderella as that may assume that there is also a handsome prince, and the client has not given me any indication that there is anyone who could fit that bill.

Geraldine: How about a general fairy story theme without referring to Cinderella?

Jethro: Ok let's see how we get on with that option...

The next task is for us to select the nouns in the case history and elect an appropriate new noun from the mapped over world...

Here's my example. I decided to use a story that reflected the fact that the client lives close to the coast...

Noun	Mapped over noun
Client	Shell collector
Partner	Deep-sea diver
Mum and dad	Cottage dwellers
House car home	Treasures
Computer	Magic shell
Men	Young divers
College	Shell painting school
Eyes, ribs	Shell collection
Safe house	distant castle
Women	Shell collectors, milkmaids, and shepherds
Job	Collecting, painting and selling shells

Baz: Just by mapping over the nouns like that, I can already see how you now have the bones to add a story to it.

Ali: I think I'm ahead with you on this. My head is already writing the story.

Jethro: That's good to hear. I must say that it is a comment I have heard before, and one of the reasons why this process is so good to use. Once you have got your nouns mapped over to a new world, then the rest can easily slot into place...

The next stage is to look at the processes in the original client history. This is why it's a good idea to highlight the verbs, as they will allow you to see the processes more clearly. In essence, your next task is to map over what is happening to the nouns so that they fit in with what is happening to the new nouns...

So let's continue and add the processes we have identified. Once again, don't worry too much if you don't get them all exactly correct. If you can map over the main processes into the new mapped over nouns you are doing well....

Met partner
Fell in love with him
Attracted to him
Allowed her to move out
Hated home
Care for them
Look after them
Studying
Spend time on computers
Stopped being with her
Became possessive and jealous
Suspected she was interested in other
Wouldn't let her
Get angry
Became violent
Started drinking
Love gone
Cleans and cooks
Demands
Hit
Violent
Wants to leave
Searching

Feelings
Too old to leave

If you look at that list, you may see that I have written the original story in a process-like manner. You can use the newly created nouns that mirror the old nouns, and then add them to the process that is listed above. When you do that, you will have the makings of a very simple metaphor story…

Once upon a time there was a young shell collector. She would spend most of her day collecting shells at the beach. One day when she was walking by the blue water, she saw a deep-sea diver emerging from the waves. She smiled at the deep-sea diver as he approached her. As he did so, she told him that she was collecting shells so that she could paint them and add them to a collection, which she could sell. When the diver asked her why she did this, she replied that she had to work hard every day as two old and cruel cottage dwellers that lived next door to her would make her leave her cottage if she didn't give them rent. The cottage dwellers owned her cottage and every year they demanded more and more rent and so each year she had to collect more and more shells. The diver was attracted to the lovely shell collector and he told her that she could live with him in his waterside cave that was filled with treasures from the deep sea.

She was overjoyed when she saw the cave where the diver lived. There were so many treasures. She was often speechless when she looked into the deep areas of the cave and saw even more bright, precious and sparkling treasures. One day when the diver was out diving for more treasures, she discovered a magic shell at the back of the cave and when she looked into the coiled section of the shell she could see amazing views of the surrounding area as if she was looking down on the countryside from above.

The deep-sea diver spent more and more time away from home. He said he was diving but he never came back with shells and his breath often smelled of seaweed wine. He became very angry and accused her of going out into the town and meeting the younger divers that were there.

She told him that all she was interested in was her shells and that she wanted to know more about shells and even go to shell painting school.

However, he refused, and one evening, when he came home, he was so angry that he smashed up all her shells. He stamped on them and broke them into thousands of tiny pieces. However, he didn't smash all of them as she had hidden her magic shell deep inside the cave.

After then, she grew older and older and never left the cave. She was afraid to go out and leave the diver even though she didn't feel any love for him anymore. All she did was to look into the shell and view the countryside around her.

One day when the diver was out, she looked into the shell and saw a huge castle. The castle had a moat and a big strong drawbridge. Inside the castle she could see it was populated with milkmaids, lady shepherds and female shell collectors like her. She sensed that this was a safe place to be and she felt that she needed to have the courage to leave the cave and go there.

She knew that soon the diver would come back again and be violent and she knew that she was getting older and weaker with each day. She also knew that the castle was a safe place for her to get away from her life with the diver....

Jethro: In order to write a good metaphor story there needs certain requirements for the story to work well. Historically, great storytellers would include these elements in their story in an unconscious way, and if they were asked "how" they constructed their story for maximum effect, they would probably say "Well I just do it without thinking; I just do what comes naturally to me". It may be that one or two of you here are natural storytellers and if so, you may start to recognise that what I am going to talk about is something you already do...

When you create the story, the story "world" you decide to use will depend on the client that you are working with. If you have a client who is very aware and intelligent then you may have to have a higher degree of abstraction when you map over into another world than if your client was less intelligent or even younger. Of course some of your clients may be 30 years old but may have a psychological age that is younger than that, so if you detect that in your exchanges, its good to bear it in mind if you are going to map over from their world to another. You may want to consider anything that the client may have given you in terms of evidence from previous communication as to where to start the metaphor. So in my synchronous exchanges with the client we discussed earlier, trains and rail transport had been part of our text exchange history.

Hag: I have a client that has a phobia of spiders, would it be good to use spiders in the story?

Jethro: Probably not, as it may not allow the client to enter the world that you are creating, and it may not be a story that is abstracted enough. Also it could be very traumatic for the client. It's a good point though, as it allows me to mention that you can ask your client in a previous email if they have an aversion to the subject you may be considering as part of your metaphor...

Richard, as I have read over your email today I found myself thinking about a story that someone once told me about a walk in the mountains. I know that the story was about snow and getting lost in the mountains. If I find that story, could I send it to you as an email some time in the future?

Jethro: That's an example I just thought of that may help you test to see if the client has any fears relating to your metaphor.

Hag: But if I were to use a monster in my story, there would be vagueness to it, as I wouldn't say that it looked like a spider.

Jethro: Yes that's right, you don't have to be too specific, you can let the client add their own imagination, and of course a monster would be there to indicate some element of fear, well at least initially...

So the first element is the act of mapping over, and once you have mapped over the nouns and the process words you will probably find it relatively straightforward to write a metaphor story...

You can even go further and embed it in a "nest" of other stories if you wish. This is where the main story nests inside one or two other stories. Being able to cut and paste will allow you to do this in a few minutes...

In this model too, you can add other therapeutic elements. Here are two that I tend to utilise, you may know of some others...

When "telling the story" the therapist can change the focus of the story by using the word "you". The best way to show this is with an example...

The old lady walked down the drive of her house for the last time. She knew she was leaving her home for good. She looked over to the right at her beautiful red and yellow flowers. She looked over to her left and saw the neat and tidy lawn. And you know when you feel anxious about moving on to new ways of living, well she had that feeling, but this time she also knew that her new found skills would allow her to be safe and secure this time.

Mark: So when you used "you" it was a way of momentarily shifting the focus from the old lady to the client.

Jethro: Yes Mark, and if you do that in a section of your story, you should be able to send a message to a client in a subtle way...

If you are not going to solve the clients' problems in your story, its worth considering that the client can have choice, and creating choice is a good way of assisting the client to move on. Again, here's an example...

Now I'm not sure what happened to the shell collector. It may be that she decided to stay with the diver, or it may be that she waited until she felt strong enough before she made the journey to the castle...

Geraldine: I see that this can still allow the client to have options and that the story can highlight that sense of choice for the client.

Jethro: Yes, and if you can add more than two options that's the best way as only two choices is a dilemma...

Let's assume that I have already written a story about going to the city and shopping...

Let's also assume that I have written a story about an old book shop...

I can use those two stories to nest either side of the story about the shell collector that we just started to create....

Man: Can you explain a little more please?

Jethro: Yes of course, perhaps a diagram will help.

Start of story 1 – shopping in the city

Merge it into the start of story 2 – the old book shop

Write the entire story about the shell collector and add any other therapeutic messages at this point.

Conclude story 2 – the old book shop

Conclude story 1 – shopping in the city

Here's an example...

The shopping in the city story – start of story 1

One day when the sun was shining I decided to go into the city with my close friend on a shopping trip. My friend was after some new clothes, but I was hoping to find some old seashells, as I wanted to decorate an old lamp I had in my garage. As the two of us both wanted different items to buy we had a coffee together and then decided to go our separate ways for about an hour and meet up again outside the coffee bar later...

The old bookshop story – start of story 2...

As my friend vanished into the crowd of shoppers I decided to venture into the older part of the city, as I knew that there would be a better chance of me finding some old shells there. I knew there were quite a few bric-a-brac shops in the old part of town.

Eventually I found myself walking down an alley, and the sounds of the shoppers started to fade out of earshot. I saw the sunlight fall away as I walked further into the shaded part of the alley. I was attracted to an old rusty iron sign hanging above a shop on the side of the wall.

I stepped into the shop and was hit by the musty smell of old furniture and carpets. The floorboards creaked beneath me as I looked at the old books, vinyl records, photograph albums, broken tennis rackets and old guitars.

I heard a coughing sound from the rear of the shop and then an old man with a grey beard and a kind smile walked into the room.

He told me he was the owner and asked what I may be interested in.

I told him that I was interested in looking at old seashells, as I had wanted to use them to make something with them.

The old man shook his head and told me that all the seashells were usually bought up by a shell collector that lives nearby. He then pointed to a large leather chair and beckoned me to sit down, saying that he would like to tell me a story about a shell collector that he once knew.

I was curious to see what the old man would say and so as I wasn't due to meet my friend for a while, I sat down in to the creaky leather arm chair with the brass upholstery pins around the arms of the chair.

He sat down in a similar chair opposite me and cleaned his spectacles with a white cloth.
He then placed his spectacles back on his head, cleared his throat and began to talk to me in a gentle tone...

The shell collector story...

Once upon a time there was a young shell collector. She would spend most of her day collecting shells at the beach. One day when she was walking by the water, she saw a deep-sea diver emerging from the water. She smiled at the deep-sea diver as he approached her. She told him that she was collecting shells so that she could paint them and add them to a collection, which she could sell.

When the diver asked her why she did this she replied that she had to work hard every day as two old and cruel cottage dwellers that lived next door to her would make her leave her cottage if she didn't give them rent. The cottage dwellers owned her cottage and every year they demanded more and more rent and so each year she had to collect more and more shells. The diver was attracted to the lovely shell collector and he told her that she could live with him in his waterside cave that was filled with treasures from the deep sea.

She was overjoyed when she saw the cave where the diver lived. There were so many treasures. She was often speechless when she looked into the deep areas of the cave and saw even more bright, precious and sparkling treasures. One day when the diver was out diving for more treasures, she discovered a magic shell at the back of the cave and when she looked into the coiled section of the shell she could see amazing views of the surrounding area as if she was looking down on the countryside from above.

The deep-sea diver spent more and more time away from home. He said he was diving but he never came back with shells and his breath often smelled of seaweed wine. He became very angry and accused her of going out into the town and meeting the younger divers that were there.

She told him that all she was interested in was her shells and that she wanted to know more about shells and even go to shell painting school.
However, he refused and one evening he came home and was so angry that he smashed up all her shells. He stamped on them and broke them all into thousands of tiny pieces. However, he didn't smash all of them as she had hidden her magic shell deep inside the cave.

After then, she grew older and older and never left the cave. She was afraid to go out and leave the diver even though she didn't feel any love for him anymore. All she did was to look into the shell and espy the countryside around her.

One day when the diver was out, she looked into the shell and saw a huge castle. The castle had a moat and a big strong drawbridge. Inside the castle she could see it was populated with milkmaids, lady shepherds and female shell collectors like her. She sensed that this was a safe place to be and she felt that she needed to have the courage to leave the cave and go there.

She knew that soon the diver would come back again and be violent and she knew that she was getting older and weaker with each day. She also knew that the castle was a safe place for her to get away from her life with the diver..

Use of "you"...

And you know how it is when you know you have to do something that is right for you even though it is painful, well the shell collector had that feeling and she knew that she had to find the courage inside herself to do what was right for her, to keep her safe, to keep her protected, to allow her to be happy again..

Use of choices...

And I don't know if that shell collector was able to make the choice that was right for her. I'm not sure if she stayed in that abusive relationship or whether she found the courage to find safety and a new life, or whether she used her skills to do something different but I do know that people still think of her and talk about her in stories, even to this day...

The old bookshop story – conclusion of story 2...

And at that point the old man looked up at me as if he had been reading the story from an invisible book on his lap. He smiled and told me that I was welcome to come back to the shop anytime I wished. I was suddenly aware that time had appeared to stand still whilst I was listening to his voice, and so I thanked him for the story and ventured out of the shop into the alley way which was now lit with sunlight.

I walked towards the sounds of people and traffic in the main street and looked back at the shop one more time before I stepped into the noise and bustle of the city centre...

The shopping in the city story - conclusion of story 1...

When I got to the coffee shop, I saw my friend standing outside holding his newly acquired shopping. I looked at my watch and noticed that the hour had passed ten minutes ago and that I was late to meet him. I apologised for being ten minutes late and told him that I hadn't managed to get any shells. However I didn't tell him that I had discovered some other wonderful things that are still with me today.

Man: I can see from the way you have structured that, just how easy it is to construct a seemingly complicated story.

Ali: Yes, it's much clearer for me too.

Jethro: So, I'm glad that you can say that this method can help you to start the process of constructing stories, so that you can deliver a message to a client as a reading cure. Of course as this is a skill, you will find that you will increase your abilities as you work with this tool and get feedback from them. In my experience, the feedback you will receive will pleasantly surprise you.

Chapter 10.

To be or not to be?

Jethro: Good morning. I hope you have all recovered from your night off...

I'm assuming that you all spent a few hours reading over all our previous work before going out and having fun?

Mark: Of course we did. It was a lovely night.

Jethro: Mark, that's a fascinating response that I wanted to elicit from you as it illustrates wonderfully how text exchanges can be confusing. I wonder if there was a hint of sarcasm in your response.

Mark: Well yes, after working all day yesterday and knowing it was our night off, I think we all made the most of our night off and didn't look over the previous stuff.

Jethro: That's great, and of course there is a detention for not doing your homework and a merit for being honest, so they have cancelled each other out, providing you give what I have just said your full attention.

Mark: I'm all ears.

Hag: In that case, I'm glad I can't see you LOL.

Jethro: I would like you to consider your response "of course we did" and to remember that when you are working online, there is no tonality....

When you are having synchronous text exchanges, you may have the tonality in your head, in other words, you will probably run an internal dialogue, that has inherent in it, the tonality that you believe you are using when in communication with the client, but in fact, the client will only have the text to go on and not any tonality, so therefore may not be able to tell if you are being sarcastic or not...

Now I'm not suggesting that you use sarcasm with your clients, but there may be other elements of communicating with them that you may not communicate correctly due to this phenomenon. I would like you to bear this in mind when you are communicating.

Geraldine: Yes, what about rhetorical questions?

Jethro: Yes, that's another possibility. How do you let your client know that you asking a question that is intended to let the client know your thought processes, without making it a question that the client feels they have to respond to? There's no need to answer that by the way...

So before we start on our main topic today, I just want you to consider that...

When you are communicating to a client by text only, the internal tonality of your own voice that may be there when you construct the text, may not be there when the client reads it.

Hag: Yes, that's a good point, I feel that I have had some miscommunication problems with clients and they may have been caused by what you have just said.

Jethro: Consider this statement...

The meaning of the communication is in the response it elicits...

When working as a therapist it's worthwhile to consider the outcome of the communication. You may have a meaning, which is what you intended to communicate, but in fact the receiver of the message can react in a different way.

Mark: Often with disastrous consequences.

Jethro: Yes, so you may wish to consider that the response to your communication will define the meaning for the receiver. Often as a therapist, it's important to understand another person's perspective and to understand first before being understood later.

Mark: It's about taking responsibility for what you write.

Jethro: Okay, so let's just go back to what Mark said at the start of today...

He also added "it **was** a lovely night"...

Well today we are going to explore a specific use of language in communicating, we are going to have a look at the verb "to be" and how that can affect the way people communicate when they are working online...

Mark said "It was a lovely night" and he used the verb "to be". Of course, from a grammatical point of view, there is nothing wrong in that, but today I would like us to consider the impact of that verb, on how we communicate. I would like to ask you, what you think would happen if the verb "to be" were removed from the English language.

Ali: That would be very difficult.

Jethro: Did you intentionally use the verb to be then?

Ali: No, LOL, I just did it naturally I guess.

Jethro: I understand that to stop using the verb "to be" may be difficult for adults that have used the verb for many years, but I would like you to rephrase what you said without using that verb.

Ali: Well instead of saying, "That would be difficult" I could say, "I would find that difficult".

Jethro: Yes, that's a good way of rephrasing it. So how does that new statement feel when you compare it to the initial statement?

Ali: Well when I said, "that would be difficult" I felt that there is no personalisation or ownership to that statement; whereas when I said "I would find it difficult" It felt more personal as it communicated how I felt.

Jethro: Okay, thank you for that feedback. Any more comments?

Man: "I wouldn't be able to do it" was my initial internal response but as that response had the verb to be in it, I changed it to " At the moment, I do not feel skilled enough to do it" and as I did that, it changed the way I felt about mastering this new skill.

Jethro: Again, that's good feedback. So perhaps if I said that getting rid of this verb might reduce confusion, misunderstandings, clarify meaning, improve relationships and more, then that would sound like quite a statement. Let's have a look shall we...?

Let's focus on the part of the verb "to be" that gives rise to identity. I am talking about the "is" part of the verb as well as the "isn't" bit too...

The leaf is green

The man is a great therapist

The dog is silly

Also...

The dogs are barking again

We are happy now

The therapists are clever

I have also produced a list where I have taken out the verb "to be"

The leaf is green

The leaf appears green to me

The man is a great therapist

The man has great therapeutic skills

The dog is silly

I perceive the dog acting in a silly way

Also

The dogs are barking again

I hear the dogs barking again

We are happy now

We feel happy now

The therapists are clever

The therapists use skills that make them appear clever

Mark: This is fascinating, or should I say "this appears fascinating to me". In fact as I said that, I realised that when I said "this is fascinating" and then changed it to "this appears fascinating to me", that other people in the room may not share my opinion that it "is" fascinating. It felt liberating in some way. I became aware that this really felt like I was communicating from my model of the world and I knew it.

Okay, can we proceed...?

Climate change is here

Scientists have used data to state that that weather patterns behave differently now to 5 years ago

Climate change is not here

Scientists have used data to argue that current weather changes will not stay this way over the coming years.

Fred is miserable all day

Fred looked miserable to me all day yesterday

I am saying this for the last time

 I will tell you this for the last time

Jazz is better than classical music

I prefer Jazz to classical music

The robber was wearing a mask

The robber had a mask over his head...

You may wish to consider how a client may use this verb in the way they communicate to you. Here is a section from a synchronous text exchange. Of course you can "be" aware of this verb and the impact it may have in both asynchronous and synchronous work, but you may have to be reasonably skilled at removing the verb "to be" in your communication when working synchronously, as you will have less time to respond than when using asynchronous email exchange...

My husband is an unfaithful husband. He is totally immoral.

Hag: well bearing in mind our previous work, the questions I would use, as a response would be...

How do you know he is unfaithful?

Jethro: Yes, that's a viable response. However I would like you to consider how you could respond and take out the verb "to be". If you have more choice in the way you work with the client then you will have more skills too...

Client: My husband is an unfaithful husband. He is totally immoral

Therapist: I can hear that you believe that your husband behaves in an unfaithful way most of the time. Perhaps you may have shifted your focus onto a belief that he behaves unfaithfully to you and have not looked at any other ways that he may behave in a moral way with you?

And...

Client: People get mistreated every day; I guess it's just the way of the world

Therapist: I notice that you believe that everyone gets mistreated every day. I wonder if you could look back at what you wrote and consider that you may have exaggerated that a little? Let me know. As you went on to say that "it's the way of the world" I wonder if you see it that way.

Client: When I was younger I was told to keep a diary and now I can look back and see how stupid I was then.

Therapist: So, some years ago, someone instructed you to keep a diary. I hear that you now feel that some of the things you wrote in your diary may seem stupid to you now. What a wonderful way to realise that you have learned new beliefs as you have grown up.

Client: I am useless when it comes to relationships

Therapist: I wonder how you would feel if you said to yourself "So far, I feel; that I have not had a lot of success when I have dated women" or "I do much better when I have women as friends than in a romantic relationship".

Hag: Those responses seem to have an in-built person centred feel to them. Could it be that by removing the verb "to be", there is a tendency to be more person-centred when the therapist is replying and omitting the verb?

Jethro: Well, that's a fascinating comment. Perhaps you could talk to some therapists that have a strong leaning towards a person centred approach and find out. Or you may be able to look at some emails, with the client's permission of course, that person centred counsellors have written.

Man: So the process sounds like you observe when the client uses the verb "to be" and then feedback aspects of what they have written and take away the verb in your response.

Jethro: Yes, that was what I did in the examples. And of course you can also use the other skills in conjunction with deleting the verb in your response. You can challenge deletions, distortions and generalisations. You can focus on their beliefs and you can use the verb to be or not to be if you wish. That is the question!

Man: LOL. I was thinking about those "big" questions. Those that that are impossible to answer, like what is the meaning of life? And why am I here?

Jethro: Go on please.

Man: Well I feel that if the verb "to be" were removed from those "big" questions then a question like "What does life mean to me?" would be less scary.

Jethro: Well I think I know what you mean. Perhaps the word scary is probably a little strong here but I can see how those questions with the verb "to be" included do seem to feel more "stuck" to me, and as I have said before, unstuck-ness is much more preferential to stuckness...

Here's a section of an email with "to be" included and then the same passage with the verb "to be" taken out...

With "to be"...

It was good feedback when you said that you were stupid as you typed out the letter to me. I guess that when you were putting your fears down in a written form they did look a little odd. I remember I had anxiety when I was in my early 20s and as part of the process I was encouraged to keep a diary. When I looked back at that diary ten years later, I actually laughed to myself at how ridiculous some of my beliefs were. I can understand why you were feeling depressed. I know these things are ridiculous but I also know that they can seem real at the time. I guess our work is to make them seem more ridiculous perhaps? That way perhaps there is a solution.

Without "to be"..

It felt like good feedback to me when you said that you felt stupid as you typed out the letter. I guess that when you get around to putting your fears down in a written form they can look a little odd. I remember suffering from anxiety when in my early 20s and as part of the process, my therapist encouraged me to keep a diary. When I looked back at that diary ten years later, I actually laughed to myself at how ridiculous some of my beliefs seemed at the time. I can understand why you may have felt that way. I know these things can seem ridiculous but I also know that they can seem real at the time. I guess our work together could make them make them seem more ridiculous perhaps? That way we may find a solution.

Man: I can see how the second response, although it is different in the words I would choose, could make a positive difference if the verb "to be" were removed or reduced. I like it and will bear it in mind.

Jethro: So we have looked at how this small but very special verb can alter how people can perceive the world in which they live and write. I hope that now you all have this new insight, you will again, consider what we have discussed today and consider incorporating, or not incorporating, that verb in your responses. You now have the choice.

Baz: This has made a lot of sense to me as I feel that by taking out the verb "to be" in my replies to a client, I feel that I will be a lot less judgemental in my future responses.

Jethro: Thanks for that, and thank you all.

Chapter 11

Where,what,how,why,who?

Jethro: Good to see that you have all managed to log on in good time today. Has anyone got anything they would like to comment on from the work we have done so far.

Baz: Yes I have a question that relates to the work we have done on how to get the client to respond.

Jethro: Yes, please share it with the group if that's ok with the others.

Hag: Yes, I'm happy with that.

Mark: Me too.

Ali: Yes.

Man: Yes I'm ok too.

Geraldine: Yes please go on.

Baz: Well, I recently received some feedback from a client that I had been working with in an asynchronous way. The feedback I received was generally good, but the client commented that some of my questions seemed a little too critical...

The client went onto say that when I cut and pasted the client's words and fed those words back to the client in my reply, I was being critical...

Of course that was not my intention, but I was highlighting the client's exact text and feeding it back to them as a way of linking back what they had said, to my reply.

Jethro: You mean like this...

Client: I work so hard to get the right results but I get so anxious and am so hard on myself that I seem to sabotage all the good work I put in. Recently I worked on a project and was late handing it in because it just never seemed good enough, and yet when I got feedback, the feedback was that it was good work.

Therapist: I noticed that you said...

...but I get so anxious and am so hard on myself that I seem to sabotage all the good work I put in. It just never seemed good enough.

I wonder if you may feel that your work has to be perfect?

Baz: Yes that's what I did, and the client saw it as a criticism because I used her own words.

Geraldine: I didn't see it that way but I can understand that as we are working with text only, the client may read it as a criticism.

Jethro: Baz, what do you think you will do differently next time in order to reduce this possibility?

Baz: Well I have written a section that I think I will introduce into my first email reply.

Jethro: Do you have it now?

Baz: Yes, would you like me to send it?

Ali: Yes please I'm interested too.

Baz: Here it is...

One of the ways I like to work is to reply to aspects of your letter by cutting and pasting your words in my reply to you. This is my way of "feeding back" what you have written so we can work on it together. I thought I would let you know that in advance.

Man: I like that. I've not had any negative feedback based on the fact that I also cut and paste the clients' work and give them feedback, but I will consider it, or at least a version of that.

Jethro: Yes, I like that too.

Hag: Thanks Baz, an idea shared is an idea stolen.

Baz: Steal away Hag!! LOL.

Jethro: Anything else?

Mark: Well I don't think we have covered this exactly but I recently worked with a client and it seemed that they were totally capable of completing tasks and goals but they never seemed to be able to do so, a bit like your last example. I spent a few email exchanges focusing on what they could consider doing differently, but after a while, I realised that they actually knew what to do and had all the skills to do what they needed to do, but they didn't have the motivation.

Geraldine: That must have been frustrating for you Mark.

Mark: Yes it was, I felt that I had "lost" a few valuable email exchanges, as I had been looking at the wrong aspect of the work.

Jethro: This seems like a case of knowing where to focus when working online. I wonder if you were focusing on the "how" rather than the "why"?

Ali: Can you say more please?

Jethro: Yes, perhaps we can have a look at a model that could represent what is present when you are working face-to-face...

And remember this is a "model" and I would like you to bear that in mind. You may wish to consider it a template for looking at the similarities and differences between asking questions face-to-face and asking questions online...

When you have your first face-to-face meeting with a new client, what do you notice?

Mark: Well for me, it's the way they look, and the way they are dressed, their appearance.

Geraldine: And they way they sound when they speak.

Man: And smell!!

Jethro: Yes I agree, sometimes a person can bring into the room a certain "scent".

Man: Nice or otherwise.

Ali: Well it's all in the eyes, or should I say nose, of the beholder LOL.

Jethro: So we notice their world as we experience it. The hair, clothes, accent, smell of perfume or tobacco, perhaps even the touch of a hand in a handshake.

Hag: Oh so different from working online.

Jethro: Can you continue?

Hag: Well when a person works online, we don't actually get to experience their environment much. We cannot see them, the hair, movement, smell etc.

Jethro: So when working face-to-face, we know that their environment is the hair, clothes, accent, smell of perfume or tobacco, perhaps even the touch of a hand in a handshake, what is the online environment? I know we may have touched on this before but this time we can expand on it to help you gain an insight perhaps into where to work with your online client.

Man: The online environment is one sided because the client cannot experience the therapist in AKOG, just the V modality.

Jethro: So you are saying that hearing, smell, touch and taste are all absent.

Man: And the V that represents the visual element is only derived from the assumed environment, what the client and therapist imagine is there.

Jethro: Do go on Man.

Ali: Hey you sound like a hippy LOL.

Jethro: No, that would be "do go on Maaaan" ☺ Sorry, Man, please continue.

Man: Oh it's not a problem, as you were talking I was able to remove my embroidered afghan style coat.

Ali: So you are a hippy LOL.

Jethro: I get what you are saying here, that there is an assumed environment that the therapist and the client have about the "other" in the relationship. When working face-to-face, both share the same environment with regards to the surroundings and both have a full VAKOG of the other, if all the senses are used.

Geraldine: So the online environment is – the words and nothing else?

Jethro: Well type of font, size and colour would be the shared "real" environment and that is visual, but there is also that "assumed" environment of the other, such as a room, lighting, computer, furniture, the things that have to be there for the process to take place, even though they cannot be seen by the other person, I'm sure that's the same for asynchronous as well as synchronous work.

Hag: I know we have looked at this before and how it relates to rapport building but how can it help with knowing where to work with a client?

Jethro: Well if you wanted to ask a question that was to be directed at the client's environment, what question would you ask?

Mark: Where is my coffee?

Hag: I'm assuming that's Marks answer and not a real question.

Mark: LOL, yes I'm saying that if I want to ask a question about a client environment I would say "Where?"

Jethro: Yes, so would I.

Geraldine: I agree with that too.

Jethro: Well let's go onto another aspect of what we are discussing. When you are face-to-face with a client, after you have met them, what else do you notice?

Baz: What they say and what they do in the room.

Ali: Yes, how they behave when they interact with each other.

Man: So when working face-to-face, the therapist can see what the client is doing and visa versa. Of course when working online this behaviour cannot be seen as there is no body language, no movement and so we cannot see behaviour online.

Jethro: Are you sure about that?

Ali: Well the text is the behaviour isn't it?

Baz: The words, the sentences, the paragraphs, they must be the behaviour for both therapist and the client, and they are common to both parties.

Ali: And also there is the unseen behaviour, I call it the **off platform** behaviour. This is the behaviour that the therapist and client are actually doing when engaged in synchronous, and to some extent, asynchronous work. This cannot be seen by either of the participants. I also feel that there is also an off platform environment too, the environment that the client and therapist do not know is there.

Jethro: That's an interesting term and concept. Yes I believe that is worth considering. All you have to go on when it comes to being able to connect with the client's behaviour is the text, the words, the sentences and the paragraph, and yet both parties know that there is unseen behaviour too. What question would you ask if you wanted to focus on a client's behaviour?

Ali: Well I would say "What are you doing", so I'm guessing that "What" is the question that elicits a client's behaviour.

Jethro: Yes I agree...

So let's move onwards towards considering the clients' skills and their capabilities, how does a therapist notice the client's skills when working face-to-face?

Mark: The therapist can "see" how well the client does "what they do", in the room. How good they are at listening and speaking. How attentive they may be and how they use empathy and paraphrasing etc.

Jethro: And online?

Mark: How skilled they are in the choice of words, the actual words they use, the actual sentences, the actual paragraphs and how they are all chosen, constructed and laid out on the page. I think that could be the equivalent of the client's skills online.

Ali: And working synchronously, how quickly they can type and reply. And also there is the element of those off platform skills too, what the client and the therapist cannot see with regard to how skilled the other is. I also feel that some skills would be off platform too.

Jethro: Yes Ali and Mark, I agree that those aspects are some ways to determine the client's skills and capabilities online. Isn't that different from working face-to-face?

Man: Yes, it seems so much more limited.

Jethro: And the question that would focus on skills and capabilities?

Mark: Well it would be "How well they do something", so it must be "How?"

Jethro: So if you ask "How" questions, the question will go to their skills and capabilities....

We have looked at the Environment, Behaviour and Skills of the client and therapist and how they are perceived when working face-to-face and online. How can you tell someone's values and beliefs when working face-to-face?

Geraldine: I guess you can't. I mean they cannot be externally observed, unlike environment, behaviour and skills, they cannot be seen.

Hag: And so I guess they can only be picked up in the client's language, which makes detecting values and beliefs in a client very similar when working online to working face-to-face. I guess it's about finding out what's important for the client and listening to their "this means that" and "this causes that" in their words or what they type as well as what is really important to them.

Ali: So beliefs and values share a common theme when working face-to-face and online.

Jethro: And the question that will elicit the values and beliefs of a client?

Hag: Well I'm thinking of how we used the "What's really important to you" question before when we were talking about values and beliefs, but I'm not sure if the question is "What" because I see how that could elicit behaviour.

Jethro: Well Hag, we may have to ask a " What" as a prior question before we ask the question that goes to values and beliefs, which is the "Why" question.

Mark: Mmmm..the client I spoke about earlier. He knew "What" he had to do and "how" to do it and I spend sometime focusing on this with him. It took a while for me to realise that a "Why don't you do this" may have been a good question to ask him. I feel that "Why" questions are the ones that go to values and beliefs.

Jethro: So let's look at this example...

Therapist: What's really important to you?

Woman: To be a good mother to my children.

Therapist: And why is that important to you?

Woman: It's important to me because if I am a good mother my children will love me and care for me when I'm old.

Hag: I have worked in a certain way where I was taught not to ask "Why" questions.

Jethro: Yes I understand that asking "Why?" may be confrontational and yet, it is a good way to work towards what motivates a client and to elicit their values. Also when you ask "why?" you can get the "because" response and when you have the "because", you will have elicited their belief as the reply would probably come back as a "this means that", or a "this causes that", and then you can work with the responses accordingly. The "How" question is about skills and the

"Why" question is about motivation and I think that relates to Marks original question.

Mark: Yes I can see that now.

Jethro: And how is the identity of the client perceived when working face-to-face?

Ali: I think that the client will say words like... Who are... or, I am a...

Man: For instance "I am a therapist" being an identity statement.

Jethro: I agree.

Hag: Yes, I feel that my identity is connected with "Who" I am.

Jethro: And when working online?

Ali: It's that verb "to be" here. I can see how the use of the verb "to be" is linked to identity. "I **am** a car driver", seems very "identity" whereas "I drive a car" is not about identity but about behaviour.

Jethro: Yes I agree. Any other comments?

Geraldine: How we can use this? I'm getting impatient LOL.

Jethro: In a minute I will give you all a summary of what we have been discussing, and then hopefully, you will be able to learn the skill of working with it. How well you do that will of course be related to how skilled you are but let me ask you this question. What do you see as "sprit" or "spirituality" and how does that show itself face-to-face and online.

Ali: Ommmmmm Ommmmm LOL.

Man: Now who's the hippy LOL.

Baz: Well I guess that means a lot of different things to a lot of people, isn't it so individual that it's impossible to define?

Hag: Well I like to see spirituality as not about God but about Oneness.

Geraldine: For me it's about something that is greater than me.

Mark: Yes, I like that. It's something or someone more important or greater than me, and that could be my child.

Jethro: Would the concept of spirit as something or someone that is greater or more important than the individual be a good definition?

Man: I like it as it applies to whatever the "someone" the "is".

Jethro: And how does it express itself face-to-face and online? Any difference?

Mark: Probably not.

Baz: Well a spiritual person can dress and speak in a certain way.

Mark: But that's really about environment and behaviour I guess.

Jethro: Any other comments?

Baz: Yes, now I think about it, I agree.

Geraldine: So when people are referring to the spiritual aspects of themselves, they may have to refer to something else that is more important or greater then themselves, and that's done by language again, or in online work, in text.

Jethro: So, let's summarise what we have discussed...

Environment

The "Where" question

In face-to-face communication – The clients' "world", where they are and live, how they look, their clothes, their surroundings.

Asynchronous communication – The client can see their own environment but they have to assume the therapists environment and visa versa. Shared aspects of the environment are the text style, the font used, choice of colour. The "off platform" environment that is unknown.

Synchronous communication – as above

Behaviour

The "What" question

In face-to-face communication – What they do, their body language and movement, their voice tone.

Asynchronous communication- The words, sentences and paragraphs. The language predicates used. The "off platform" behaviour that is unknown.

Synchronous communication – as above

Skills & Capabilities

The "How" question

In face-to-face communication -How well they do something, measurement of skill, degrees of skill.

Asynchronous communication– skills in using words, their choice of words, sentences, paragraphs and layout as well as typos. The "off platform" skills that are unknown.

Synchronous communication – as above and also including speed of response.

Beliefs & Values

The "Why" question

In face-to-face communication –Why? Why should I? Why is it important for me? Expressed in language as "this means that" and "this causes that"

Asynchronous communication- as above

Synchronous communication- as above

Identity

The "Who" question

In face-to-face communication –Who? Language based "Who" and "I am"

Asynchronous communication – text based use of "I am" in text- use of the verb "to be".

Synchronous communication- as above

Spirituality

The "Who else" question

In face-to-face communication -Who else? – out there- others- greater than me. Language based.

Asynchronous communication – as above, text based

Synchronous communication – as above, text based

Ali: So from this summary I can see where working face-to-face and working online has differences and similarities.

Jethro: Yes, and now we have started to explore this model we can consider some other aspects of it too…

Firstly, you can now see how the – Where, What, How, Why questions can help you to go to the point where you feel you need to go to, when working with a client. Also you may wish to consider this concept regarding the model too..

If you want to facilitate a change, then you have to work with the client at a point that is the same or "above" the level that the client perceives the problem. Of course these "levels" are not strictly levels in the sense that they physically lie on top of each other but as a model its worth considering the level as such..

Spirit
Identity
Beliefs and values
Skills and capabilities
Behaviour
Environment

Ali: I wonder if it could be that the level of "off platform" communication, decreases, the higher up the levels we go?

Jethro: Ali, another interesting point that you could consider.

Baz: So if the client has a problem at the behaviour level, I won't be able to get the client to make changes by focusing on the environment as that's a level "below". I need to work on the same level or a level above.

Jethro: Yes that's usually the case, unless the client believes that their problems are at one level (Identity), when in fact, they may be at a lower level (behaviour). This model also allows us to let the client know if they are confusing their identity with their behaviour, a common error...

Client: I am a bad mother.

Therapist: So you say that you are not too good at behaving like a good mother?

Client: Well yes I guess I was never taught properly.

Therapist: So, you could consider learning some new skills.

Client: Yes I could.

Therapist: And when you have learned new skills...

Geraldine: Did you go down to the behaviour level then?

Jethro: Yes I did, because on this occasion I was letting the client consider the option that her stuckness wasn't really at the identity level but at the behaviour level and then I moved up a level to skills after that.

Geraldine: Yes I see that.

Jethro: Go on.

Geraldine: It seems that making a "shift" in the environment is for example, much easier than making a shift in the clients' Identity.

Jethro: Yes, so that's why in the above example I moved the focus from identity to behaviour and then worked at the level above behaviour, as it's easier to make that shift for the client. Focusing on the identity level as a way of facilitating change is more difficult that, for instance, the environment.

Man: Yes, that's a good model to bear in mind for me because now I'm thinking that it can be applied to many areas of work.

Jethro: Have a look at this example...

Client: I am just not going to be able to be a best man at the wedding. I can't do that speech.

Therapist: (recognises that the client feels he is not capable of doing the speech and decides to ask a question at a higher level – values). How important is it for you to do this speech?

Client: Well it's very important for me as I have known the groom for 20 years but I worried that I won't do a good job.

Therapist (recognises that the client is focusing on how skilled he feels he needs to be and so replies at the values level again) I wonder what's more important here, is it for you to be seen as a highly skilled entertainer or to be at the side of your close friend?

Client: Yes I hear what you say.

Therapist (moves to a higher level – identity) And do you feel you need to be an entertainer or a best friend?

Client: Yes I guess being a best friend is the thing here.

Jethro: Well that's a rather spontaneous example but I hope you can see how you can use this model to recognise the level that the client is "at" and then using that knowledge to respond so that the client can make changes.

Mark: It's certainly something I will bear in mind in the future and I was just thinking how I could use this in an email by sending the "levels" to a client so that they could use them to help identify where they need to focus.

Jethro: Like this Mark...?

In your environment, I wonder what you would like to be different.

And what behaviour would you like to be different in that new environment?

And what skills do you need in order to carry out these behaviours in a way that's right for you?

And what will you have to believe about yourself in order to support your new skills?

And what will be important to you?

And can you fill in this sentence? When I have achieved this I can say to myself that I am a...

And who and what else that is important to you will be affected?

Mark: Yep, you beat me to it.

Jethro: Well take some time to consider what we have explored in this session. And when you realise that you have been able to utilise this model in your future work, feel free to let me know.

Chapter 12

Online hypnosis?

Baz: It looks like we arrived here before Jethro today.

Mark: Yes he's not here yet and as we are having an open session today, I wonder if we are meant to talk amongst ourselves as to what we want to discuss?

Baz: Hmmm, yes I'm not sure.

Ali: Perhaps that's why Jethro isn't here yet.

Jethro: **HERE I AM!!**

Ali: Whooo, I thought you were not going to turn up today.

Jethro: Sorry I was late to log on. I can see we are all here now.

Man: Yes I'm here and I can be **BIG and BOLD** too.

Mark: **Me2**, bigger and bolder LOL, and I was thinking about the way Jethro changes the way he writes to us when he's ending some of the sessions.

Man: Yes I think we have commented on that before, what is going on there?

Jethro: I was intentionally making my closing paragraphs vague.

Geraldine: Can we have a look at some from previous "meetings"

Jethro: Let me go back and put some of the old paragraphs up here so we can look at them.

Jethro: Ok, and well done for noticing all those language patterns. We have already explored how to recognise distortions, deletions and generalisations in text and how to respond to them. What we haven't discussed is this...

When a person uses a combination of distortions, generalisations and deletions, the language will become unclear and increasingly vague. The language becomes "hypnotic".

Ali: So if we use a combination of those patterns we are using hypnosis online.

Jethro: Simplistically stated, yes we are. Also your client may use a lot of those patterns in their emails to you, so in fact, they are already "hypnotised".

Hag: How interesting. So in your ending paragraphs, you used a combination of language patterns; deletions, distortions and generalisations to hypnotise us?

Jethro: Well I would rather say that I intentionally used those patterns so that when the "client" reads them, the client will give meaning to the sentences that is right for them...

Let me construct a longer closing paragraph so you can explore further...

So John, I know we have explored many things today.... Many people have used the online process to make changes in the way we have started to do so...And as we explore more... then **so you will learn more about yourself**... And making changes means that you will be able to look back on these exchanges and **realise new learning along the way...** And of course every time you learn a new thing about yourself... **you can apply it in new ways**...This is one of the most important aspects of working this way...things may be better...And I'm not sure if you will reply to me tomorrow or at the end of the week...but my old trainer once told me that once you have mastered something, its impossible to forget how to fail...and as you

make this a useful experience...I'm wondering if you would prefer to work by email or chat next time?

Man: In your example above I can see that you have used deletions as you said " we have explored may things today" and yet that does not explain what those "things" are, so that's a deletion.

Mark: And the second line uses the words "changes" and "process" so that's two nominalisations there.

Geraldine: I can see a "this means that" in the line "Making changes means…"

Baz: And a generalisation too "Every time you learn a new thing about yourself", Oh and the word "thing" is a deletion too.

Hag: I can see that you have also done a few other things with the language here too. It's more than a combination of deletions, distortions and generalisations, for instance...

Some of the text is in **bold.** Is that intentional?

Jethro: Yes Hag, it is intentional. Lets call it **digital marking.** By highlighting areas of text, you can embed areas of text that you would like the client to pay special attention to. If you were working face-to-face with a client, and wanted to embed some information so that the client paid attention to it, you may do that by emphasising your voice at that moment. Of course when using text, that's not possible, so the other way to do that online is to use **bold text.** Here are some examples of how this can be done...

Well John, I understand from your earlier email that you have made some **significant changes** already in the way you relate to what you call "difficult people". When you have **mastered the skills we have explored,** perhaps **you will email me** and let me know how much it's helping you.

I understand that you have said that there may be some issues that you are not **ready to talk about** just yet. It's fine for you to not **write to me about those things** until **its right for you. Now** we can carry on as before until you feel that **you can discuss what you want.**

Hag: I can see there that you have highlighted areas where the client has **done well** or **made changes** and areas where you may want the **client to act** upon.

Jethro: Yes, you can use these lines as openers...

When you...

If you...

You may consider...

What would it be like for you when...?

Baz: So can we use hypnosis online?

Jethro: If a person can read text and become engrossed in that text, then I'm sure that by using the above examples, a client will be able to attach meaning to what you have written that is right for them. And if that's hypnosis, then the answer is yes.

Man: But perhaps not a good idea to use this way of writing in the entire body of text, but to use it at the start of an email or at the end?

Jethro: I can agree with that. Any questions?

Hag: Yes, I noticed too that you said in your example "I'm not sure if you will reply to me tomorrow or at the end of the week".It seemed that you were giving the client a choice.

Jethro: Well in a way it was more an **illusion of choice**. My goal was to let the client know that I want them to email me back, and in the sentence I said that they could email me tomorrow or at the end of the week. What I was really communicating was that I wanted then to email me back.

Hag: So if I said, "Do you want to have fun now, or later ", the message is that they will have fun.

Jethro: Exactly. I also used a "quote" when I said, "My old trainer once told me..." This can allow you to deliver a message to a client that would be useful for them to hear but you do not want it to come from you, so you use a "quote". This makes it more difficult for the client to reply with a "Yes, but..." response because it is an indirect message to them...

For example...

A wise old man once told me that...

Some experts often say...

Geraldine: Isn't some of this a little like brainwashing?

Jethro: Well I often get asked that question and my response is that these skills and new ways to work with a client online are very powerful. For that reason they require a great deal of integrity from the therapist in the way they are used. Naturally I wouldn't like to see email going out to a client that said...

John, now I know that **you have done so well** you may find yourself thinking that you may want to **pay twice as much for your sessions** from now on..

Jethro: The process is the same but the outcome is different and so how you use these skills is all about integrity and working within professional boundaries...

How about an overview of these language patterns?

Mark: Yes please.

Ali: I was going to say the same thing.

Jethro: OK. Here are the major patterns that you can use if you wish to use hypnotic language patterns. You can use these patterns if you want to allow the client to make sense from what you write, in a way that's meaningful for them. They will attach meaning to it.

Mind reading – the ability to know what someone else is thinking or feeling.

John, I know that you have been curious about how you can be more assertive and in this email we can work on that...

This means that and this causes that – the belief that one thing means another or that one thing leads to another.

John, as you have filled in your mood diary and emailed it back to me then I guess that it means that you have been able to experiment with the way you have been thinking...

John, I can understand that you have not been too happy this week and it may be that your recent email has allowed you to put your feelings into perspective again.

Generalisations – words that state absolutes.

John, I'm sure that you always consider your family in such circumstances...

John, I don't think that anyone would disagree with you about how you must be feeling.

Can do – Words that suggest that something is necessary or possible.

John, it's possible that after practice you will be able to look at this in a new way.

Nominalisations – Verbs that have been turned into nouns.

John, I can hear that you are aware that confusion can lead to greater understanding and a reduction of fear.

Deleted verbs, nouns and comparative deletions.

John, we have explored many things today in our text exchanges.

John, I can hear you like to learn and perhaps that is what you have done today.

John, it seemed that you were able to grasp my points even quicker.

Quotes – Making statements that assume they were made by others.

John, my old Zen master once said that anxiety is something to look forward to.

Digital marking and instructions- bold text to highlight meaning or suggestions for the client.

John, now that you have been able to express **how good you are feeling. Now,** I wonder if you could use that feeling to think about how you could **act differently after reading this email.**

Covering all possibilities – statements that cover all of what is possible.

John, I wonder if you will quietly think about this for a day or so before you talk to your partner, or will you do it today?

Use of "And" – The use of "And" assumes a link between what you have previously written and what you are currently writing. This can only work well in synchronous communicating...

John: I feel that's all I have to say on the subject.

Therapist: Do you feel we have covered a lot today?

John: Yes I do.

Therapist: And so John...

As we come to the end of our session...

And as we have explored...

And expressed our feelings...

Ali: As I read that last example I could see how that would be a good way to end with a client when working synchronously. I can see it can allow the therapist to "wrap up" all the discussions in the session, and to allocate a "meaning" that's special for the client.

Hag: I have been thinking about this session and I believe that I have been using hypnotic patterns without realising it.

Jethro: Yes, that's an interesting point Hag. You may wish to look over your old emails and see if you have been working hypnotically, without knowing it. You may wish to consider that when you know the difference, what difference it could make to the way you work. And of course when working synchronously, it's worth remembering that the client is in the here on now. Whereas when working asynchronously, they may be reading your email days after you have written it. Even so, I do feel that there is scope for this type of language at the end of emails.

Ali: It's an interesting model.

Jethro: Thanks for that Ali. I'm glad you used the word "model" just then, as I wanted to discuss briefly the concept of a model for online therapy. Our work together has explored avenues that show how NLP based theory and practice can be incorporated into both asynchronous and synchronous exchanges. They show one "model" of working online. If you are working as an online therapist, you may wish to go back to the emails you have previously sent out and see if you have developed a model in the way you work.

Hag: I have already done so and noticed that I tend to use a model that incorporates a lot of hypnotic language, without recognising it as that.

Mark: And I use a lot of "confirming" what the client has written by recognising their words in my response to them but I don't consider any outcome for them.

Jethro: I hope that you may be able to look at your previously sent emails and see where you could incorporate some elements of this NLP based model...

We have learned a lot today, and as we integrate our new learning into our work we can allow ourselves to let this experience make all our choices better still. And we can consider how we will use this way, to work with integrity. And we may use it synchronously or asynchronously. You have all said how you want to increase choice in the way you work. You may have trained in one model or another, but as you start to use some of these powerful skills, you may let each new discovery shape the way you work in the future...

Thank you all.

Chapter Thirteen.

Working synchronously

Example of working synchronously with a client.

Here is an example of a therapist working with a client synchronously. As you read the text and the response, you can also read the additional notes that let you into the thinking behind the questions and the statements in the intervention. For this work I have indicated the client as "C" and the therapist as "T".

C: Well now we have made contact I'm not sure if this is a good idea.

Therapist notes use of deletion "this" and decides to uncover the deletion.

T: What is it that you think is not a good idea?

C: The whole concept of working online.

Therapist notes an element of all or nothing thinking from the client in the use of "whole" as well as possible belief from client that some aspect of working online will mean that it is not a good idea for the client. Therapist responds by asking directly whether client has a belief about working online.

T: So what leads you to believe that working online may not be a good idea for you?

C: Because I can't see you, it is weird.

Therapist notes that client uses verb "to be" by stating that it "is" weird and notes that client's belief is in the format of a complex equivalence namely "because I can't see you it means it's weird". Therapist feeds back the possible complex equivalence to the client, using the word "because" instead of "means" to match the client's use of the word.

T: So you are saying that you believe that working this way may not be a good idea for you because you cannot see me.

C: I'm not sure.

Therapist notes a slightly longer pause here in the client's response but does not comment on change of response speed. Therapist responds by reframing the client's complex equivalence and therefore their belief.

T: So does that mean that a blind person could NEVER have counselling or therapy because they wouldn't be able to see the therapist.

C: Ha, that's funny and you know, I never thought of it like that.

Client responds with humour and a declaration that his perceptions of the belief may have shifted. Therapist considers another reframe.

T: And of course, there could be many advantages to me not being able to see you.

C: Well, yes I didn't get around to having a shave this morning LOL.

Client takes up the thread before the therapist and adds his own reframe that gives a positive outcome of having the belief. Therapist suggests a shift to propel the client to an outcome frame.

T: So, perhaps we could "see how we go" and agree to 3 sessions and then have a review.

C: Yes, that seems like a good idea.

Client is in agreement Therapist starts with outcome question "what do you want to get?"

T: So John, I wonder what you would like to get from our time together.

C: Well I have problems with my girlfriend.

Client states a problem space regarding his girlfriend. Therapist notes the presupposition that the client has more than one problem and responds using the word "problems". Also therapist notes a deletion with the use of the word problems and decides to uncover what the "problems" are

T: And what sort of problems do you have with your girlfriend?

C: Well I'm not so sure. I could tell you about what comes directly to my mind.

Client asks permission to give an example Therapist agrees.

T: Yes ok, do continue.

C: It's my girlfriend.

Client uses deletion "its" and therapist decides to uncover the deletion by asking what "it" is

T: What is it about your girlfriend?

C: OK. Well she's always telling me that I am lazy.

Therapist notes all or nothing thinking "always" and responds with an example of a reframe that states what must be true if she is always doing that.

T: So she "always" tells you. Could it be an exaggeration on your part? I mean, she's not telling you that you're lazy now is she?

C: LOL...no she's in the garden.

Client sees humour in the response and provides evidence that the use of "always" on his part is not true.
Therapist reiterates what must be there for the all or nothing statement to be true.

T: Well I thought I would check, after all, I can't see you, so she may be standing right behind you and telling you that you're lazy.

C: Well she tells me I'm lazy, usually when she wants the house tidying or if she wants to go somewhere and I want to stay in and watch TV.

Client gives example of when his girlfriend tell him he's lazy Therapist asks client what his girlfriend is doing as a way of opening up discussion around the word "lazy".

T: And what is she doing in the garden at the moment?

C: Well she's lazing on a sun lounger, chilling out and that's what pisses me off. It's fine if she wants to relax but when I want to relax, she gets on my case. Last week she told me that all her friends think I'm a waste of space too.

Therapist notes that girlfriend is on sun lounger and considers using the word "lazing" in his response to highlight that his girlfriend may carry out similar behaviour to him, but asks for clarification instead. Therapist also notes all or nothing statement "all her friends" as well as the mind read, "her friends think I am a waste of space" Therapist asks permission to feedback overview to client, and uses the permission to decide on what section of the client response to reply to.

T: So can I just take a minute to get my head around this?

C: Sure.

Client agrees. Therapist questions girlfriends mind read.

T: How does she know that all her friends think that you are waste of space?

C: Well she did tell me that they don't like me.

Client responds with mind read "they don't like me" Therapist uncovers mind read by asking client "how does she know".

T: How does she know that they don't like you?

C: Well she said that once when she went out on a girls' night out, I was the only person who didn't pick up their girlfriend

in the car at the end of the night. She got the bus home and their partners collected the others.

Client does not directly respond to the question. Instead he gives an example. Therapist seeks more information about his girlfriend's response.

T: And how did your girlfriend feel about that?

C: She said she felt neglected as their partners collected all the others, and she had to make her own way home.

Client gives feedback on what his girlfriend said to him about what happened and how she felt. Therapist realises that the response didn't uncover the mind read so the therapist asks again.

T: And then her friends told her that they don't like you.

C: I guess so.

Therapist is aware that client may be making a guess and suggests this option.

T: I wonder if you are guessing?

C: How do you mean?

Client asks for clarification and therapist replies, making it clearer by stating, "did they specifically tell her that?"

T: Well how do you know that her friends don't like you? Did they tell specifically tell your girlfriend that.

C: Well I'm not sure.

Client responds with uncertainty and so therapist suggests that the client's girlfriend may be mind reading.

T: Well does that mean she could be assuming that they don't like you.

C: Well she could?

Therapist notes that the client has made a statement but used a question mark. Therapist decides to not enter into whether the response was a statement or a question, but moves towards instructing the client about how he could learn to challenge a mind read from his girlfriend.

T: Could you find out?

C: How?

Client responds by stating he may not have the skill to find out and asks how. Therapist states that in order to find out, the client could ask her.

T: Well could you ask your girlfriend?

C: Oh no! I couldn't ask her that.

Client responds with a limitation in the form of a modal operator of possibility "I can't do that". Therapist decides to open up the limitation by suggesting the possible option that could happen if client were to get out of the problem.

T: What would happen if you did ask her?

C: Well she may get angry.

Client responds with his belief of what may happen in the form of a cause effect "Asking her would make her angry". Therapist asks client to expand on this assumption.

T: And what would make her angry.

C: She would think I didn't believe her.

Client responds with a mind read "she would think..." Therapist questions mind read.

T: How would she know that you didn't believe her?

C: Because I had to ask the question.

Client responds with the word "because", forming a complex equivalence "because I have to ask it means I don't believe her ". Therapist decides to feedback this belief back to the client in that format.

T: So you're saying that when you ask your girlfriend a question, it means that you don't believe her.

C: Well in the past it has meant that, and that's what I want, I want my girlfriend to believe me.

Client responds by stating what he wants. Therapist notices that this outcome is not well formed as the outcome is not about the client but about his girlfriend. Therapist decides to move on towards working with the client goals.

T: So John, can you give me a list of what *you* want and we can have a look at it.

Therapist uses italic lettering to emphasise word "You" in order to shift the focus towards the client.

C: I want to get on better with my girlfriend......

Therapist notes the comparative deletion "better" but does not reply as client is using dots ..... to indicate he is still sending.

C: I want to have more confidence.....

Therapist notes that client uses nominalisation "confidence" but does not reply as client is using dots ..... to indicate he is still sending.

C: I don't want hassle from my parents.....

Therapist notes that client's outcome is not well formed as it states what the client does not want and it is not stated in the positive, but does not reply as client is using dots ..... to indicate he is still sending.

C: I want my girlfriend to believe me when I ask her a question.....

Therapist notices that this outcome is not well formed as the outcome is not about the client, but about his girlfriend but does not reply as client is using dots ..... to indicate he is still sending.

C: Erm..that's it for now.

Client states that he has completed his outcomes list and the therapist asks the client to decide where the best place to work together would be.

T: John, lets have a look at what you want, I wonder which one of those items would have the most positive effect on you.

C: That's easy, I want more confidence.

Client responds and uses the nominalisation "confidence". Therapist responds by asking the client about any sensory evidence he may have that will let him know when he has achieved his goal and also denominalises the nominalisation " confidence" to the denominalised form "confident".

T: And when you are more confident, how will you know.

C: I'm not sure.

Client responds but is uncertain so therapist explains more about sensory specific awareness.

T: Well what will you be doing differently...what will you see...hear and feel?

C: I guess I will be able to deal with my girlfriend and my parents more.

Client uses unspecified verb "deal", and also the comparative deletion "more" The therapist asks the client for further information and fills in the comparative deletion by stating "better than you are doing now"

T: In what way would you be able to dealing with them better than you are doing now?

C: I would be able to ask them questions and I would be able to say no to them.

Client gives response that indicates a behavioural change that the client would see as achieving his goal. The therapist asks the client to decide which of the two options (girlfriend or parents) would be the option to consider first.

T: So do you find it hard to ask questions to your parents as well as your girlfriend?

C: It's more difficult to ask my parents questions.

Client responds by stating that he finds it more difficult to ask his parents questions than asking his girlfriend. Therapist considers the possibility of responding with "all questions?" but decides to ask for more information.

T: In what way?

C: Well I never ask them questions....just cant.

Client responds with all or nothing statement "never" and also uses a modal operator of possibility "he cannot ask them questions" Therapist decides to respond to modal operator and ask the client what would happen if he were to move out of his problem.

T: And if you did.

C: Well...I don't know...it's just that when I was a kid, my dad said...don't ask it's rude... so many times.

Client does not give direct answer but refers to a belief that his father had. "If you ask questions it means you are rude". Therapist notes this complex equivalence and asks the client for more information.

T: Can you expand on that?

C: Well often at a meeting when the boss says "any questions" I feel that I can't ask a question as I feel that I'm being rebellious and rude.

Client refers to a recent event where he felt that asking a question meant that he would be rebellious and rude. Therapist decides to use reframe response by feeding the belief back on to himself.

T: So do you think I am being rude?

C: No why?

Client responds with a negative and asks for clarification. Therapist responds by stating that he has been asking questions about the client.

T: Well I have asked you so many questions in this session, dozens in fact.

C: Yes that's true.

Client agrees. Therapist uses a reframe again to indicate another outcome that might have been if the questions were not asked.

T: And can you imagine how different this session would have been if I hadn't asked any questions?

C: Well it would have made the session ridiculous.

Client agrees by stating that it would have been ridiculous. Therapist responds with a reframe in the form of a mini-metaphor.

T: And someone told me that when the Titanic was being built, one of the engineers thought that there was a problem with the design of the ship but he never asked the question.

C: Are you serious?

Client asks if the story is true and therapist admits that it was a metaphor.

T: Well no I'm not, I was just thinking of a metaphor to float the point home.

C: Well it did seem a bit of a stretch but I can see what you're driving at...there are lots of professions that thrive on asking questions.

Client agrees that the metaphor may have been too far fetched to be true but agrees with the therapist that many professionals ask questions. Therapist gives examples of professionals that ask questions.

T: Yes, my doctor asks me questions, so do the police.

C: It is odd that I've always considered asking questions to be rude.

Client indicates that his belief about asking questions may have changed as he says that he now sees his old belief as "odd". Therapist asks him to clarify his belief now. Therapist notes that the client used the all or nothing form for "questions", indicating "all questions" and not "some questions".

T: And do you now?

C: Well I don't, no, not now.

Client states that his belief has changed regarding asking questions. Therapist asks if the client can take the new belief into a behavioural change.

T: And so what's the first thing you could do differently as a result of this session today.

C: Well I could try and ask questions.

Client says that he will "try" and ask questions but his response is not contextual so therapist asks the client to put his new behaviour into context.

T: To Whom?

C: My girlfriend and my parents for a start...oh and my boss as well as other professionals.

Client states that he will attempt to change his behaviour with specific people, Therapist also gives the opportunity to ask him a question.

T: Do you have a question for me?

C: Erm...yes, can we arrange our next session?

Client responds by asking the therapist a question. Therapist notes this behavioural change and makes a note to ask for feedback regarding his behavioural change at the next session.

Chapter Fourteen.

Working Asynchronously

Example of working asynchronously with a client.

Email construction.

Below is an example of how the contents of this workshop can be used in the construction of asynchronous emails.

In the First email sent in from client "Paul", I have allocated numbers in brackets that relate to areas for comment in my response back to him. For instance, if I detected, from Paul's initial email, that he was prone to "mind reading" in his text, then I have allocated a (3) in Paul's email. This number then relates to "mind reading" in the key list at the end of this section.

I have also used the same system when replying to Paul's email to indicate how I have addressed these areas in my response.

First email from Paul.

Jethro,

I would like support as I am lonely but I'm not sure why I am writing to you (1) I'm scared. Scared of always (2) being alone. I feel (13) isolated from everyone (2) else, even when I'm with friends. I feel (13) this because, no matter who they are, or what they do, it seems everyone (2) can find someone.

Everyone (2) but me. I've never (2) had any kind (2) of relationship with a girl. And if I do seem to be making a connection with anyone (2), there's always (2) someone else they are thinking about (3). It's always (2) me being rejected, never (2) the other guy. People (2) tell me that I shouldn't worry. Some days I feel (13) like crying, but I can't summon the tears. Other days, I feel (13) like something's building up (1) that wants to explode from out of me. But every (2) day, I wake up with the same feeling; alone and cold. There never (2) will be anyone (2) for me. I don't want to be alone and yet I cannot see (13) a way out of this. I want there to be someone there for me. (4) Someone I can hold. Someone to loves me like I love them. (4).

Paul.

First reply To Paul

Hello Paul (1)

Thanks for your first email to me. I'm glad you could take the time to sit down at your computer and write to me. (1)

Having read over your email, I felt (13) quite saddened (1) by the desperate tone of your words. You described to me, only too well, that you felt (13) numb, isolated, apathetic and emotional.

I can understand (1) that if you feel (13) this way that you may want to break down and cry. It feels (13) a natural response (1) to feeling (13) so negative about yourself and your situation.

I noticed that the second paragraph on your email, the one where you mentioned in quite some detail how you felt, (13) that you had used quite a lot of what I call " all or nothing words." (2)

Here are a few from your email to illustrate what I mean. (2), (22)

I'm isolated from **everyone.**

Everyone can find someone.

Everyone but me.

I've **never** had **any** kind of relationship with a girl.

It doesn't look like **anything** will change.

It's **always** me being rejected.

Never the other guy.

If your words reflect the way you see yourself and the world around you, then I would like you to consider that you may do a lot of **all or nothing thinking**. (2) In other words you see (13) the world as black/white, win/lose, everybody/nobody, always/never.

If you do this a lot, (and your email suggests that you probably do) then you will see (13) a world that contains no "in between" areas.

So I would like you to consider the concept of all or nothing thinking. (11)

I would like you to go back to those statements and consider how those situations are in reality

For instance, do you feel really isolated from *everyone?*

Perhaps you could look at your statements and try changing them, so that they become more realistic and rational.

You may wish to get back to me with your thoughts on this. (11)

Paul (1), you also wrote in your opening lines that you felt (13) that you were not sure why wanted to write to me. It may help us both if you could think about what you would like to get from working together. (1)

One way to start our work together is for you to give me some information about what you would really like to get from working together with me.

One way to start this is for you to do a little exercise. (11)

Can you create a set of "lists" under the following headings? (4), (16)

A list of things* you have in your life and want to keep
 – This is the "I am grateful for" list

A list of things you have in your life but you don't want

A list of things you don't have in your life but you want

A list of things you don't have in your life and you don't want
- This is rather odd, I like to call it you "fear" list

- NOTE. The "things" can be anything that comes to mind –
  people-friends-family-objects **as well as aspects of yourself,**
  so if you have a sense of humour and want to keep it, then put
  it in the first list.

Hopefully this may give us a blueprint where our work needs to be
focused.

Well Paul, (1) there seems quite a lot there for you to consider and
when (5) you reply back to me on 25th May at 3:00.p.m, you
may be able to enlighten me a little more regarding what you would
like to get from our time together. (5)

It feels (13) good to have made a start (1)

Regards

Jethro

2nd email from Paul

Jethro,

Thank you for your reply. You mentioned that my method of thought was very all or nothing. I hadn't noticed that before and it was quite a shock to me. (6)

I'm (12) a logical person and I work in accounting. I have realised that I will often say a word like "nobody" when in fact it's not actually true. At work I said "nobody will want to do that" but in fact three people in the team actually wanted to do the project (6). With regard to me feeling isolated. I was being very rational and realistic when I said I'm always (2) being rejected. I've been on dates with girls, but every time (2), without fail, they've turned me down for someone else. The last time I went on a date I became very angry after the night out. I saw her looking at another man at the bar and then I knew that even though she was with me for the rest of the evening, she was thinking about the guy (3). It made me very angry and when I confronted her about it, she became defensive (9) and we never dated again. The reason she dint get back to me was because I'm so useless at dating.(10) I love my job but because I don't have a girlfriend I can't go (8) to works functions and that's so frustrating. I am (12) useless.

Here's my list

What I have and want to keep (7)
My intelligence
My friends
My family
My good job

What I don't have but want
Someone to love me (4)

What I have and don't want
Anger (14) at others that have a happy relationship (14)
Loneliness

What I don't have and don't want
Cancer
Bankruptcy

Intrigued into what you have to say next,

Paul.

2nd Reply to Paul.

Hello Paul (1)

Thank you for writing back and letting me know that you have given my comment about "all or nothing thinking" some thought. It must have felt quite a surprise (6) when you first realised (6) your all or nothing thinking may not "always" seem correct ☺ (6).

It's good to get that feedback that you have started to notice that you have done some all or nothing thinking. (2) Perhaps you may have created some "all or nothing sentences" whilst you were writing to me?

Have a look over your recent email and see if you can spot any? Feel free to let me know if you do. (11).

Perhaps you could go back and look at them in a new way, and see if you really have experienced "always" feeling (2) rejected. (11).

From what I read, it seems that you said that you do have friends (7) and that you enjoy your job (7) and probably have similar accounting skills (12) to those you connect with. You probably have a common bond with them through work. (7) I read that you recently felt that you couldn't attend a works function because you didn't have a girlfriend to take with you. I wonder what would happen if you did do to the function by yourself. (8).

Paul (1) I wonder if you could tell me what you think would have happened if you had gone to the function by yourself. (11).

It felt like a very upsetting experience for you when you (1) ended your recent date after an argument. It seemed that the evening was going well for you until she looked at someone else. You wrote that she was "thinking about the guy" (3) after that.

Paul (1), I would like to you have a think about this question and reply to me in your reply if that's possible. (11).

I wonder how you knew that she had thoughts of him? (3), (11).

Of course I can totally understand how you may have felt (13) if that happened (1) but I wonder if it was possible that you **assumed** this. Of course I may have made an inaccurate observation, so please get back to me and let me know.

You said that she became defensive and you said that at the time you were confronting her (9). I notice that you have focused on her "defence" but I wonder if you could consider how you "confronted" her instead.

I wonder what you actually said? (11).

I can understand that you may feel that you are not as capable as others at relating (14) to some women. Of course your experience may have been less about your abilities but more about her desire to have a conflict free "first date". Can you imagine how the world of relationships would be if everyone blamed themselves 100%, if they didn't "hit it off" at the first meeting? (10)

Finally Paul (1), you mentioned that you "wanted someone to love you" as one of your outcomes. I understand that you would love to have the skills to relate to some women and I wonder...

How realistically do you believe this outcome under your control? (4).

Could you rephrase that sentence so that you have more control over achieving your goal? (11).

Paul (1), I hope my email will allow you to **explore further how you think, and how you can make changes**. I understand that learning new skills can take time and I'm sure that you have experienced times when you have learnt new accounting methods that you didn't always get right the first time. Of course as **you build on what we have started, you may hopefully incorporate your new learning as you have done so before. (15).**

Look forward you reading your next email.

Regards,

Jethro.

3rd email from Paul

Hello Jethro ☺

I have started to realise that I do a lot of "mind reading" (6) and this week I realised that I do it a lot when I'm with a woman. I was at work and one of the new women in the team said to me "We make a good team as I am good at the creative side and you are good at the organising". After she went away, I said to myself
"She's only saying that because she wants my job". A few seconds later I said to myself "I'm mind reading here", (6) and that made a big difference to how In was able to relate to her after that. (6)
However when I was out in the evening, playing tennis, I saw her drive past the tennis courts with my boss in her car. This made me very angry, as I "knew" that she was only with my boss because she wants to get promotion over my head. Will I ever be able to stop mind reading? On a plus though, I have felt that I have not been doing so much "all or nothing thinking" and I was able to pick out the ones in my last email to you. (6) You may notice that there are less in this one ☺ ☺. (2)
I started to think about what it would be like if I had gone to the works function by myself. My first though was "people will think I am a loser "and I smiled ☺ when I spotted that mind read. (6)

I understand what you meant when you asked about my outcomes being sensible. If I want someone to love me, I understand it's not about me but about them. (4) In the past, if I didn't feel that they loved me, I would feel anger. (14) That anger would grow and then my relationship (14), (9) would go wrong (I was going to write " go ALL wrong there but I stopped myself as I now believe that it wouldn't have gone ALL wrong, just my part in it and how I am)(6)

I feel that may have been placing demandments (14) on my dates and wanting instant love. Oh and the woman who I work with (Zoë), she was in my bosses car as they are car sharing. I asked ☺ (16)

I feel I have started to move on and yet I have so much frustration
(14) as I can often get it wrong.(17) Oh and by the way, I said to my last date that she "was only with me so she could meet other men ". Of course now I feel silly when I write that.

Where to next?

Paul.

3rd Reply to Paul

Hello Paul ☺ (8)

Wow! (1) It does seem, from your email that you have started to recognise quite a few aspects of how you used to think and behave. (18). From what I read about how you recognised that you had done some "mind reading", it appears that you have already started behaving in new ways (18).

As I looked over your email, I didn't notice any "all or nothing" sentences so I hope that's a sign that you have started to get the hang of seeing other options in your thoughts and how that affects your behaviour differently. (18).

From your email I also became aware that you might be having a different view on how you may relate to women as you said...(22)

I feel that may have been placing demandments on my dates and wanting instant love.

Paul, (1) I wonder if you could tell me that when (21) you go on another date, what you might DO differently next time? (21).

Perhaps you could consider that and get back to me next time? (11).

Of course you did say that you felt that Zoë is only with your boss so she can get a promotion, but then you asked her and she said she was car sharing. How did you feel when you received that response from her? (1).

It does seem that you may set up a belief about something and then not challenge it.

If you notice yourself mind reading, you have two options (5), (16).

The first is to say to yourself "I'm mind reading" and my mind read may not be based on facts.

The second way is to "ask".

For example...

She's thinking about someone else.

Question "Are you thinking about someone else?"

Paul, you said that you felt that getting angry (14) would cause (9) you to not to relate to women you dated. I wonder if it's not so much about getting angry but more about believing your own mind reading that's affecting how you relate to women you date?

Many years ago (17) my old piano teacher once told me that one day I would play one tune with my left hand and another tune with my right hand. I tried and tried but I could not play two separate tunes at once. Until one day, after a lot of practice... after a lot of mistakes and getting it wrong. And you know how it is when something just clicks into place?

Well now I can look back on how I felt then and realise that it takes time and practice to learn a new skill.

Paul. I know that you may still be considering the works function and wondered if you had decided to **go and enjoy the evening by yourself? (20).**

I know you have gained many insights into how you can think and behave differently. (15).

I wonder if you could **get back to me (5) and let me know if you original goals have changed.**

Could you tell me what you want from our work together now? (11).

Has much has changed for you? (19).

Looking forward to **your reply (20), (5)** next week.

Warmest regards,

Jethro.

Key.

Build and maintain rapport (1)

Note/respond to all or nothing thinking (2)

Note/respond to mind reading (3)

Note/respond to well-formedness in outcome (4)

Set up response frame (5)

Note/respond to client's awareness change (6)

Value client's resources (7)

Note/ respond to "can't do" (8)

Note/reframe belief in the form of cause effect (9)

Note/reframe belief in the form of complex equivalence (10)

Suggest tasks for client (11)

Note/respond to use of "to be" (12)

Match predicates (13)

Note/respond to nominalisation (14)

Hypnotic language (15)

Provide info to client derived from cut and paste database (16)

Provide suitable metaphor for client (17)

Presuppose problems are in the past (18)

Check behaviour change (19)

Digital marking (20)

Presuppositions about future (21)

Font matching (22)

Remove verb "to be "in reply (applies to entire response)

Chapter Fifteen.

More exercises and writing tasks.

These examples are some of the writing tasks that I have used when working online. They are not all strictly from an NLP concept as some have a Solution Focused element to them. I have included these, as I feel that NLP is solution focused in its approach, and shares a lot of common ground with the solution-focused concepts.

Blame or aim

This exercise works well using email exchange but it could be used synchronously in a "questions and answers format". The purpose of the exercise is to allow the client to see and feel the difference between two styles of thinking and the difference in outcome that can derive from each thinking (and writing) style. The exercise asks the client to consider the **SAME** problem or issue in two different ways.

John. I would like you to write back to me regarding the problem we have previously discussed. This time I want you to consider the problem and answer the following questions.

In the first example, John, I would like you to respond to the following questions and as you do the writing, you may also want to add at the end of the section how you felt after completing it.

What is the problem?

How long have you had it for?

Why did the problem happen?

What haven't you solved it yet?

Who is at fault?

John, now I want you to consider the SAME problem and reply to the next set of questions. Again, at the end of the section you may wish to add how you felt after answering this set of questions.

What do you want instead of the problem?

How will you know when you have achieved what you want?

How can it be solved?

Who can help you reach your objective most quickly?

What resources will help?

What can be learned from this experience?

The miracle question.

This writing task can allow the client to use their imagination to consider their future in a new way. It works well when exploring goal achievement and so is useful in early sessions. It can be used in both synchronous and asynchronous settings and allows the client and therapist to identify any solutions that may arise from answering the "question". It can allow the client to describe in writing how their life will be different once the problem has been solved or managed in a new way.

John, I want you to consider the following. Imagine that when you go to sleep tonight, a "miracle" happens and all the problems that you have mentioned have disappeared. As you were asleep, you did not know the miracle had happened. However, when you wake up, what would be the first signs that let you know that the miracle has happened? What do you notice first? What do you see differently around you? How are you behaving differently? Can you think about this exercise and write back to me regarding what will be different for you?

Ripe old age.

This writing task, which also works well synchronously and asynchronously, can also allow the client to consider the future and "look back" on how their life would be like if they 1) Were able to solve the problems 2) Not able to solve the problems.

John. Let's suppose that it's the future and you have lived to a ripe old age of 90, or older. Now you are looking back on your life. What would your life have been like if a) You had not sorted out this problem and b) You had sorted out this problem? You may wish to write out both scenarios and let me know how it felt to approach them.

Wise old you

This is similar to the exercise above and works well in both synchronous and asynchronous modes. This exercise can allow the client to imagine they are "old and wise" and can give advice to "their younger self" on how to solve the problems.

John... I would like you to imagine...that you have lived to be 90... or even older...imagine that for a moment...could you tell me...what advice or guidance...would you give to... **YOU NOW**...about how to get the best...through this difficult situation...to sort out things for yourself...to gain more control over your life...?

How did you get there?

This exercise works well using an asynchronous working style. It can be a useful tool when working on goal achievement. It uses the approach of presupposing that the client has **already** achieved his/her goals, and then it asks the client to explain how they achieved them.

John. I wonder if you could consider the following. You said that you wanted to be free of the problem we have discussed. I would like you to imagine that you have **NOW ACHIEVED THAT GOAL**. I would like you to write back to me and let me know **HOW YOU MANAGED TO ACHIEVE THAT GOAL**. What did you do? What did you do first? What were the stages?

Teach me how you do that?

This exercise is your way of modelling "how" the client "does" certain behaviours. It can be effective on two levels. Firstly it allows the therapist to collect a lot of information about how the client does certain behaviour or how a client achieves a certain goal (even if that goal is bothering the client). Secondly, it can allow the client to gain insights into how they are maintaining their problem and then identify how they can make changes. This exercise works well using asynchronous exchange.

John. I notice that you say that you get jealous quite a lot. Let's assume that you are an expert at "doing" the behaviour that we call "jealous". I know that's an odd way to look at it but from what you have written; it does seem that you have had a lot of experience at doing "jealous".

So John, I wonder if you could teach me how you "do" the behaviour that we call "jealous". How would you teach me to do "jealous"? What images would I make in my head? What would I say to myself? What are the steps involved? How will I know when I am doing "jealous"?

Neutral observer.

This exercise, one suitable for asynchronous work, can allow the client to write about their experience from a neutral point of view. This can allow the client to see the events in a new light and also to allow the client to start to challenge some of the assumptions about the event so that they can "see the other side" of what happened.

John. I know you have outlined what happened with your parents last month. I wonder if you could write to me again about what happened but this time I would like you to write the story of what happened "as if" you were a neutral observer. Perhaps you could imagine you were a passer by or a police officer giving evidence of what you saw happening.

You might want to start of by writing... "I was walking along when I saw...", and then continue.

S.C.O.R.E model.

This is another exercise that the client could write about in an asynchronous mode. This writing task can allow the client to break down their problem into a number of relevant chunk sizes, so that it is more manageable. It can also highlight some areas where the client can apply change. S.C.O.R.E stands for Symptoms, Causes, Outcomes, Resources, and Effects. You will perhaps notice that this model moves the client from "problem" to "solution".

John. Could you think about your problem and let me know how you can respond to the exercise below. I would like you to write about your problem under the following headings.

Symptom – What are the signs for you that indicate something is wrong? You may wish to consider the feelings that you experience or external messages you may receive from others.

Causes – What do **you** think is causing the problem?

Outcomes – What do you want instead of the problem?

Resources – What behaviour, skills, capabilities, beliefs, values and any other resources do you have that you can use to achieve your goal?

Effects – What will achieving this goal do for you? How will achieving this goal affect you over time?

Looking back over your old work

This can be a useful asynchronous exercise for a client that may be close to ending their work with the therapist. The therapist can suggest that the client looks back over all the email exchanges and provides feedback to the therapist with regard to what has worked and what work needs to be done. The therapist can suggest that the work done by both of them can also be a possible reference for the future. Perhaps the client (depending on their circumstances surrounding confidentiality) may want to compile a "book" of the work so that they can read the exchanges in the future. If confidentiality is a problem then a "book" can be stored securely online for future reference.

Chapter Sixteen.

Bibliography.

Andreas, S. Faulkner, C. (2003). The NLP 21 Day Unlimited Achievement Program. In: *NLP The Technology Of Achievement.* London: Nicholas Brealey. 303-309.

Alder, H. Heather, B (1999). *NLP in 21 days.* London: Piatkus. 13-51.

Bandler, R. Grinder, J. (1975). *The Structure Of Magic Vol 1.* Palo Alto. California. USA: Science and Behaviour Books. 39-110.

Bandler, R. Grinder, J. (1981). *Trance-Formations: NLP and the structure of hypnosis.* Moab,Utah: Real People Press. 240-250.

Bavister,S. Vickers,A. (2004). *Teach Yourself NLP.* London: Hodder. 75-82.

Bourland, D. Johnston, P. (1991). *To Be Or Not: An E-Prime Anthology.* San Francisco: International Society for General Semantics.

Bryant, J. (2007). *Online rapport.* Available: http://www.nlpco.com/library/business/rapport accessed 11th Nov 2007.

Dilts, R (1983). *Applications of Neuro-Linguistic Programming.* Cupertino California: Meta.

Dilts, R. (1990). *Changing Belief Systems With NLP.* Capitola. California: Meta.

Dilts, R.DeLozier, J (2000). *Encyclopedia of systemic neurolinguistic programming and new NLP coding.* Scotts Valley: NLP University Press. 1226-1246.

Hall, L.M. (1996). *The Spirit Of NLP.* Carmarthen: Anglo American Books. 115-136.

Jacobsen,S. (1986). *Meta-Cation.Volume 2.*Cupertino: Meta Publications. 117-118.

Johnson, R (1988). *Forty activities for training with NLP.* Vermont: Gower.

Jones, G. Stokes, A (2009). *Online Counselling: A handbook for practitioners.* Hampshire: Palgrave MacMillan. 71-84.

Knight,S. (1998).*NLP at Work.* London: Nicholas Brealey. 165-178. Kostere, K. Malatesta, L. (1989). *Get The Results You Want.* Portland. Oregon, USA: Metamorphous Press. 217-237.

Kraus, R. Zack, J. Stricker, G. (2004). *Online Counselling – A Handbook For Mental Health Professionals.* San Diego: Elsevier. 19-50.

Lankton, C.H, Lankton, S.R. (1983). *The answer within: A clinical framework of Ericksonian Hypnotherapy.* New York. Brunner Mazel.

Lankton,C.H, Lankton,S.R. (1989). *Tales of Enchantment: Goal directed metaphors for adults and children in therapy.* New York: Brunner Mazel.

Lewis, B. Pucelik, F (1990). *The magic of NLP demystified: A pragmatic guide to communication and change.* Portland: Metamorphous press. 68-112.

McLauchlin, L. (1992). *Advanced Language Patterns Mastery.* Calgary: Leading edge communications. 15-16.

Mehrabian, A. (1981). *Silent messages: Implicit communication of emotion and attitudes.* Belmont: Wadswoth.

O'Connell. B. (2005). *Solution Focused Therapy.* London. Sage.

O'Connor, J. Seymour, J. (1990). *Introducing NLP.* London: Mandala. 109-110.

Suler, J.R. (2000). *The Psychology of Cyberspace*.http://www-usr.rider.edu/~suler/psycyber/psycyber.html.Last accessed 25th Aug 2009.

Unknown. (2008). *Nominalisations.* Available: http://www.unilearning.uow.edu.au/academic/3b.html. Last accessed 26th Feb 2008.

Unknown. (2006) .*Online Networking.* Available: http://howto.lifehack/online_networking. Last accessed 11th Nov 2007.

Woodsmall, W. *So called logical levels and systemic NLP.* Available: http://www.cnlpa.de/presse/loglev.html. Last accessed 6th March 2009.

Also from MX Publishing

Seeing Spells Achieving

The UK's leading NLP book for
learning difficulties including dyslexia

More NLP books at www.mxpublishing.co.uk

Also from MX Publishing

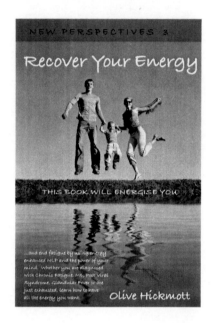

Recover Your Energy

NLP for Chronic Fatigue, ME and tiredness

More NLP books at www.mxpublishing.co.uk

Also from MX Publishing

Stop Bedwetting in 7 Days

A simple step-by-step guide to help children conquer
bedwetting problems in just a few days

More NLP books at www.mxpublishing.co.uk

Building rapport

Lightning Source UK Ltd.
Milton Keynes UK
17 October 2009

145035UK00001BA/7/P

9 781904 312741